A Mother's Grief Observed is a deeply moving account of one mother's journey, through her baby's death, to a richer life.

For those experiencing loss, it says whatever you are feeling is normal and all right—God understands.

For those who need to be called back to look at past loss, it pulls at your heart again in its cleansing, liberating view of God's personal care.

For those desiring to understand a friend's loss and stand alongside, it is an excellent source of help. (I especially appreciated the epilogue.)

For me it has been an emotional, joyful reminder of God's personal dealing with me through the deaths of loved ones.
        —Mary Lou (Mrs. Joseph) Bayly

Rebecca Faber has met head-on the greatest fear of every parent and emerged, not unscathed, but with the sweet essence of Christian hope. *A Mother's Grief Observed* is a costly perfume that will grace all who read it with the fragrance of life.

There are no bromides or clichés here. Rather, we find the radical truth of God's Word woven into a rich, spiritual biography by a young mother with the sensibilities of a theologian and poet.

This book should be read by every young parent and should be on the shelf of every pastor!
        —R. Kent Hughes, pastor
        College Church, Wheaton, Illinois

A Mother's Grief Observed is a gift from an extraordinary writer to anyone who has lost a child, wrestled with God, or struggled to understand how great pain can be compatible with faith. Rarely do emotion and insight and eloquence come so powerfully together.
        — Daniel Taylor, author
        Letters to My Children

In *A Mother's Grief Observed,* Rebecca Faber holds nothing back. Losing her precious child was awful. It hurt, and it still hurts, and she hated it. The loss stretched her faith and her marriage nearly to the breaking point, and she hides no ugly emotion. Her very vulnerability is a tribute to the memory of her son.

That's the strength of this book. You will not read it with a dry eye, and neither will you be protected from the sharp pain of grief. Shock-induced platitudes give way to grief-inspired resentments that must be dealt with in God's own waiting room. To have been any less honest in her agonizing journal would have been to minimize her loss. And by not minimizing it, she has maximized for us the faithfulness of God in the valleys of life and death.

— Jerry B. Jenkins, author
Left Behind

I was deeply moved by *A Mother's Grief Observed.* I have read many a parent's observations about grief following the death of a young child, but none has moved me more than Faber's account of what she and her husband went through following the drowning of their son William. The way Faber examines her feelings, her soul, and her relationship with God will resonate with anyone experiencing the loss of a loved one. An essential resource for any who grieve.

— Mike Yorkey, editor
Focus on the Family magazine

A Mother's Grief Observed will minister to anyone who is learning to live again after the death of a loved one. This mother's story vibrates with raw emotion even while, strangely enough, offering encouragement to others who grieve.

Through the author's intense honesty as she journeys toward God's peace, readers can see that their emotional pain is not abnormal and that they can survive a crushing loss.

This book will also help others offer appropriate comfort as they understand what grief can do to a marriage and see the power of showing God's reality through practical, caring ways.

— Sandra P. Aldrich, author
Living through the Loss of Someone You Love

A Mother's Grief Observed

REBECCA FABER

Tyndale House Publishers, Inc.
Wheaton, Illinois

All of the author's proceeds from the sale of this book will go to the William
Eduard Faber Foundation, 101 First Street, #269, Los Altos, CA 94022, and
will be used to help children in various ways.

All Scripture quotations in running text are taken from the *Holy Bible,* King
James Version.

All other Scripture quotations are taken from the *Holy Bible,* New Living
Translation, copyright © 1996. Used by permission of Tyndale House
Publishers, Inc., Wheaton, Illinois 60189. All rights reserved.

"Stop All the Clocks" from *W. H. Auden: Collected Poems* by W. H. Auden.
Copyright © 1940 and renewed 1968 by W. H. Auden. Reprinted by
permission of Random House, Inc.

Poems by Amy Carmichael copyright © 1936 by the Society for Promoting
Christian Knowledge. Used by permission.

Prayer by Betty Scott Stam, "Lord, I give up all . . ." copyright © 1938 by
Fleming H. Revell Co. Used by permission.

"Life Is a Gift We've Received" (William's Song) by Sally Rumsey reprinted
with the author's permission.

Poems and quotations by the following authors are in public domain: Phillips
Brooks, John Bunyan, Emily Dickinson, John Donne, George Eliot, Henry
Scott Holland, Christina Rossetti, Cecil Spring-Rice.

Every attempt has been made to credit authors of poems used. If anyone can
supply information regarding those for which author is listed as unknown, the
publisher will make necessary corrections in future printings.

Visit Tyndale's exciting Web site at www.tyndale.com

Library of Congress Cataloging-in-Publication Data

Faber, Rebecca, date
  A mother's grief observed / Rebecca Faber.
    p. cm.
  Includes bibliographical references.
  ISBN 0-8423-3995-7 (pbk. : alk. paper)
  1. Children—Death—Religious aspects—Christianity. 2. Bereavement—
Religious aspects—Christianity. 3. Grief—Religious aspects—Christianity.
4. Consolation. 5. Faber, William Eduard, 1991-1993. 6. Faber,
Rebecca, date. 7. Drowning victims. I. Title.
BV4907.F33 1997
248.8′66′092—dc21   96-47555

Printed in the United States of America

03 02 01 00 99 98 97
7   6   5   4   3   2

To
Patty Kern Auwerda
and
in memory of Jake

CONTENTS

PROLOGUE

William Eduard Faber died June 1, 1993.

If someone asked me what life was like before William died, where would I begin? A month before he died? The day he was born? Where?

A week before he drowned, I remember we visited McDonald's for a quick treat—my sister-in-law, Linda, was visiting us at the time. The kids were so healthy and beautiful, tumbling around in the play area. Bobby, my eldest, was six, and my middle one, Catherine, three. Bobby raced Catherine to the top of the enclosed slide, then both slithered over to William's smaller enclosure to laugh at him and cuddle and squish him. William, at eighteen months, was sturdy and square. Children of mine, all one entity, three separate parts, elastic, moving, checking up on each other, coming together, splitting apart.

Linda took several photos of them that day. They splashed a kaleidoscope of primary colors as they moved: red slide, green steps, yellow gold hair flying away, and large blue eyes twinkling irrepressibly. Mischief and energy vibrated from each little body—my big kid, my medium kid, my little one.

Trio of rubber, three walls bending away from each other, leaning back together, like a cartoon geometric that changed its shape countless times in countless ways but always returned

I do not find that this position . . .
of unbroken peacefulness and inward song
is one which we can hope to hold unassailed.
It is no soft arrangement of pillows, no easy-chair.
It is a fort in an enemy's country,
And the foe is wise in assault and especially in
    surprise.

And yet there can be nothing to fear,
for it is not a place that we must keep,
but a stronghold in which we are kept. . . .
The moment we are conscious of attack,
we look "away unto . . . Jesus, who endured."

AMY CARMICHAEL, *Rose from Briar*

to original lines and form. They defined themselves in themselves, a trinity of fun. They loved action. Bouncy circles inside the cage-climbing area, throwing the plastic balls, interrupting their frenzied play briefly to gulp their drinks, rejoining the play: slide, crawl, peek, hide. Joy-filled.

A week later, the black tunnel of William's death enclosed us.

We lived in a suburb down the Peninsula from San Francisco and were committed members of a lively church, faithful at meetings, leading a small group, helping with music. I often played the piano or sang during services. My husband, Bob, worked for a small but growing high-tech company, running their sales and marketing group.

We had met and courted in Boston, where I was a teacher in a small private school. After we married, we moved with Bob's work, first to Chicago where our two older children were born. And then finally to the Silicon Valley, computer heaven, the chip center of the universe.

Like so many families, we changed houses in the last stages of my pregnancy as we anticipated William's birth. Our previous home finally sold, and our new one was truly modern, with floor-to-ceiling windows, a pool, and the gratuitous California Jacuzzi (a luxury item I'd sworn I'd never own). With small children, we hesitated about buying a house with a pool. But the advantages of the house seemed to outweigh its imperfections.

What about normal, everyday life? Our last week holds happy memories.

We went on a camping trip, over a long weekend, with some friends from church. Great times with their kids and ours playing and laughing together in a lush, green, riverside area.

On Sunday we all took a walk that was a worship service in

itself. Quiet steps under giant sequoias—those compelling trees that enable modern man to breathe. Your lungs feel more alive, healthier, there. We loved the good air. It was clean and satisfying. Inhaling that crisp air, arrogant men wither. Respect is demanded and given.

My neck is thrust all the way back as I look up the towering, arrow-straight height. I see my small size.

The children dart from leafy green shadows into wet bark-lined clearings. It's a comfort to walk in such a fortress of natural beauty.

Our two-minute sermon that day was about fish—Jesus feeding the people from a small boy's lunch—and the other mom kindly provided visual aids in the form of small, cheese-flavored, fish-shaped crackers. The children munched on these, leaning on a monstrous log, and later scampered around puddles, ran through sticky mud, jumped clear of dripping leaves.

William was still holding several of his small fish crackers, tightfisted, an hour later. He'd eaten only one or two and, piratelike, saved the rest as booty of the day.

That weekend camp-out was fun, if damp and rainy. It's good to look back and remember.

William died the day after we returned home—a Tuesday. For nearly a year, I counted each day, cataloged each week. Looking at my calendar, there was a small red number under each Tuesday: *This is how long it has been since I have held him. This is how many weeks since I wiggled his little, sweet feet (always a kiss for each one, before the sock went on) into his long, big shoes.* He was moving from the baby-toddler stage to the small-boy stage. You could see it in the final photos of him.

Looking back now, from a great distance it seems, every

word and phrase and emotion of that afternoon is burned into my memory.

I was busy inside the house—cleaning the tents, tidying the house, sorting through wet camping gear, while feeding the children their supper. I put Catherine to bed first (although she was older than Baby Will, she did not take a nap, so often went to sleep earlier). I did not pray with Catherine that night—she was exhausted and fell asleep quickly.

I remember how tired I was, how the damp, plastic tents and wet, muddy clothing felt in my hands. I remember going back into the kitchen; I can see the California sun through the huge windows, still hot and clear after 5 P.M., and the rich, green bushes lining the turquoise-colored pool.

I see Bob, with the long poles in his hands, down at the deep end of the pool. He had come home briefly before leaving on a business trip, to clean the pool for me. He's practically standing still as he pushes first the nets and then the vacuum slowly back and forth, gathering debris, leaves, algae from the sides and top of the pool. William is in his high chair, whining quietly. I'm nearly frantic, with people arriving for a Bible study in a few hours and so much still to be done. I rush back and forth down the hallway.

William has not finished eating, yet does not want to sit in his high chair and finish his supper. No one else is in the kitchen, and he is bored all alone. Rather than listen to him whine and cry, I decide to take him out to Bob. I figure I will sit down and finish feeding him a little later.

Bob objects, begging me not to leave William with him. "I can't watch him right now."

But I overrule him. "Honey, please! I have so much to do.

Who would true valour see,
Let him come hither;
One here will constant be,
Come wind, come weather;
There's no discouragement
Shall make him once relent
His first avowed intent
To be a Pilgrim.

Whoso beset him round
With dismal stories,
Do but themselves confound;
His strength the more is.
No lion can him fright;
He'll with a giant fight,
He will make good his right
To be a Pilgrim.

Since Lord Thou dost defend
Us with Thy Spirit,
We know we at the end
Shall life inherit.
The fancies flee away!
I'll fear not what men say;
I'll labour night and day
To be a Pilgrim.

JOHN BUNYAN

Just keep him a minute while you finish vacuuming the pool. I'm doing three different things at once!"

Against Bob's wishes, I take William outside to him. Bob pleads with me, but I insist. I move William from safety, in the house, to danger, out by the pool.

I thought William would be OK. He hated deep water, even in the bathtub. He preferred to take showers with me or two-inch-deep baths. Even at the age of eighteen months, he would not jump in when Bob and I swam but had to be coaxed in slowly. Bob tried to tell me William had gotten over his fear and would need more attention than he could give just then—but I refused to listen.

I did not think about how alluring the water toys down at the Jacuzzi end might appear to a young toddler. Also, the greatest fun for William was doing something grown-up—perhaps he tried to push a stick around in the water, the way Daddy was doing, but lost his footing.

Perhaps he tried to climb the low wall beside the pool, the way Daddy does, and slipped and hit his head, falling in. Later we found a small bump on the front of his head.

I can still see Bob, with a small boy standing at his feet, in the bright sunshine of a color-studded and vibrant evening. The last time I saw William alive.

Bobby was playing in the small yard beside the deck. Our friend Amanda was sitting on the deck, cuddling her newborn baby girl. Three people were near him, yet no one saw William fall, no one heard him cry.

Two rings at once: the phone and the doorbell. I hand the phone to Amanda and go to the door. A homeless man is seeking help—we had been glad to help others in the past, giving housing, transport, food. He would later recall that as he and I spoke, he saw William go past the windows at the back of the house.

Only moments later, I hear Bob slamming up against the glass doors, trying to get in.

I had already locked up those doors, preparing for his leaving. When alone, I kept only one back door open to the yard—fewer doors to watch my kids' passage in and out.

Seconds later he is in the house, William white and limp in his arms, Bobby crying, "Daddy, is he dead?"

Bob screams, *"Phone 9-1-1!"*

"Amanda, give me the phone!" Me, trembling and dialing.

Bob trying CPR (he was formerly a lifeguard), but then rushing out the door, as I am still fumbling with the phone, shaking.

Milliseconds later, I finish with the lady at 9-1-1. Bob is gone. Bobby is nowhere to be seen. Our guest, Amanda, stays at the house (Catherine is sound asleep) and I run out the door thinking, *If I were Bob Faber, where would I go now?*

There is a fire station only eight houses away from us, but across one very large intersection. I run.

I come on Bobby at the corner where the traffic light is. I grab him and race across the road. Cars stop to let this mad lady pass; I am not going to stop for them.

People are clustered at both corners. I hear whispers, "What's wrong?" "Is something wrong?"

At the fire station, Bob is outside beside the flagpole, hands on hips, pacing. Where is William? Far at the back of the building, I see several men and a small, white clump on the floor at their feet.

That's the only time I screamed. "No!"

No. No. Don't let this be true.

Bob hushes me, fearing I am getting hysterical. I immediately gather Bobby into my lap, collapsing in front of the fire station. One small square of green grass, under a flag. The sun is still shining, and the evening air is still balmy and gentle.

"Bobby," I say gently, "if William is dead, he's with Jesus right now."

Bob objects, telling me again to be quiet.

He cannot believe it's all over. He's hoping they can revive William. He has to hope.

I whisper again, very quietly to Bobby, as I cradle him, "He's with Jesus, right now, if he is dead." My legs and arms encircle my firstborn son, warming him, holding him. Wrapping him in my love.

I would learn later that Bobby was the first one to see William dead. He had screamed to Dad as he reached in and began pulling him out of the water. William was so heavy that Bobby could not lift him fully and partially dropped him.

The hospital, the police, the aftermath are also crystal clear in my memory. At the end we were allowed to hold William, after they had done all they could for him. We stayed a long, long time with him, there in the emergency room, weeping and cuddling his dead body. People from church, dear friends from nearby, came quietly—standing, saying little. One man's deep groan as he entered and saw William's body lives in my memory today: Rich's emotion was straight from his heart. His baby boy was only a little younger than Will. His anguish came from his gut and expressed what we could not yet express.

As I held William's body, we two became one figure wrapped together, submerged in death's ocean, timeless. We were in a circle of quiet, a circle of love, a circle out of time, forever.

I'll lend you, for a little time, a child of mine, He said
For you to love the while he lives, and mourn for when he's
  dead;
It may be six or seven years—or twenty-two or three—
But will you, 'til I call him back, take care of him for Me?

He'll bring his charms to gladden you, and should his stay be
  brief
You'll have his lovely memories as solace for your grief.
I cannot promise he will stay, since all from Earth return;
But there are lessons taught down there I want this child to
  learn.

I've looked the wide world over in My search for teachers true,
And from the throngs that crowd life's lanes, I have selected
  you.
Now will you give him all your love, nor think the labor vain—
Nor hate Me when I come to call to take him back again?

I fancied that I heard them say: Dear Lord, Thy will be done.
For all the joy Thy child shall bring, the risk of grief we'll run;
We'll shelter him with tenderness, we'll love him while we may.
But should the angels call for him much sooner than we'd
  planned,
We'll bear the bitter grief that comes—and try to understand.

AUTHOR UNKNOWN

But the noises of the hospital began to invade our circle, and I forced myself to surface, to leave. I turned from the quiet embrace. I could have stayed all night. Saying, "I love you." Saying, "Go to God, little boy. Go to God." He was warm again, from all their labor over his body. But he was gone.

I let his body go, motioning to Bob to come and say goodbye. Calling for Bobby to come and hug William, one last time. Catherine was still sleeping at home. We told her the next morning William was gone.

Bob planned to go to the mortuary, but I was not sure I could. I was afraid I would freak out and scream, or go quietly insane. I wondered what good it would do. I remembered other dead bodies I had seen in open caskets, and I could not equate my warm, wiggly baby with those long, cold, white, painted forms.

I remembered hearing other people who had lost a loved one say, "It was important. I was glad I saw him." I didn't care if it was important. I didn't care about doing the right thing. I didn't think it could *help me,* not one bit. But I wondered if William would care—in a bizarre kind of way. Would he know? Did he care?

In the end, I went. I went to say to William that even if he was ugly, even if he was cold, even if he was marred by their cosmetics, I would always love him. There was no form he could take in which I would value him less. I did not go for myself. I went for him.

He was beautiful. I did not touch him—though the others did. The very air around him felt frozen and repelled me. My sister held him, talked to him, played gently with him. My brother-in-law also said farewell. That took courage. I admired them.

I did not stay long. But his beauty comforted me. And I am grateful now that I went, because I got to see his body one more time. Even if he was not there, that stiff body had been a part of him and so was very precious to me.

We held a memorial service for William within days of his death. Our dear friend and former pastor Jerry Root came from some distance to help us, to listen, to lead the service. We'd known him for years; he'd watched our marriage develop and our family grow. He loved us and taught us, when we were newlyweds, how a Christian husband and wife should behave.

At the service we sang the song "Lord, You Are More Precious than Silver." And we added a second verse that not everyone sings: "And the Lord says, 'Child, you are more precious than silver. . . .'" I can never sing that song without remembering that day, remembering my littlest son.

Bob told everyone how William was the charming fifth member in our family, an important part of our children's play and games. The two older children were proud of William and boasted of his exploits at school, at nursery. However, as much as they loved him, at times they got exasperated with the way he would gather up and hide their most interesting toys. He never quite made a clean getaway, however. He always dropped a hair bow, or Lego, or small toy behind him as he carried away his treasure, his booty.

That's how we coined the nickname for him, "the little pirate," and Bob used this characteristic of William as an example for those at the service. (For many of our friends, this memorial was a rare excursion into a church.)

"Follow the treasure," he said. "See the bits and pieces that drop here and there. . . . Read God's Book, the treasure map, and find the real booty, the entire chest of gold. Follow the treasure to heaven."

It was clear and simply said. There was power in his broken sentences, the sharing of his heart. Bob's talk was quite short, but so deep and charged with emotion that not a person moved; people hardly breathed.

My brother asked me later, "Where do you find strength? What gives relief and comfort? Please—I want to know!" He urged me to keep a journal, to write about my feelings and thoughts as I tried to come to terms with this amputation, this tearing apart of our family and my life.

And that is what I share now in the hope that it can be a tool, a small comfort, for others who are hurting. Because others were willing to tell their personal struggle and journey, I was strengthened in that first, most difficult year. A book like this allows strangers to view the most private places of one's life; but in the end, if I can help one person—*just one*—make it further, go in deeper, hold on tighter to God, then it's worth the telling.

BOOK ONE

The First
Thirty Days

Stop all the clocks, cut off the telephone
Prevent the dog from barking with a juicy bone,
Silence the pianos and with muffled drum
Bring out the coffin, let the mourners come.

Let aeroplanes circle moaning overhead
Scribbling on the sky the message He Is Dead,
Put crepe bows round the white necks of the
    public doves,
Let the traffic policemen wear black cotton gloves.

He was my North, my South, my East and West,
My working week and my Sunday rest,
My noon, my midnight, my talk, my song;
I thought that love would last forever: I was wrong.

The stars are not wanted now: put out every one;
Pack up the moon and dismantle the sun;
Pour away the ocean and sweep up the wood:
For nothing now can ever come to any good.

W. H. AUDEN

DAY One

- -

JUNE 2

This is my second day of life without my baby, Lord. Grief is an intrinsically selfish emotion. Lord, help me.

I can't believe he's never coming back, in this life.

One of the hardest immediate things is this: I miss his little busyness. The prying, mischievous fingers. The wiggly body that comes for a hug or an "Owie—kiss?" but then squirms to leave again, to run and play.

The house has been so noisy. Thank You, Lord. My arms are empty, but these precious friends have brought me their babies, and I've needed that so much.

Bob has been crying heartrending sobs, all day, as he telephoned every person who ever knew us or him. I do not feel any responsibility to tell people. It's not their grief, it's mine, and his, and Bobby's and Catherine's. Except for a very small group, I don't trust people to miss William as much as we do; and to miss him less is to say he was less precious. Of less value.

But so far I can understand and cope with his expression of grief. He needs to call out to the world that our baby's gone. Like that poem by Auden, "Stop all the clocks . . . he's dead . . ."

I am so worried about Catherine and Bobby. How can I help them? Their sorrow must have some kind of outlet . . . what? Yesterday both of them began to show signs of grief and stress. I'm so afraid I'll tell them something wrong or miss a major symptom of emotional pain. Oh, Lord, watch out for my medium kid, my big kid.

DAY Six

JUNE 7

Today I made an awful mistake. I took Catherine to the park close by, to her play group. A favorite aunt stayed with her, and her favorite playmate. I left, taking Bobby to his friend's home. Catherine fell to pieces. Why? She had all favorites surrounding her—complete security, I thought. Why? What was wrong? I had tried to set up a good, normal thing for her.

On reflection, it is easy to see why she fell apart. This was one of *her* firsts—this was her first time at a park without Will. How blind could I be? Of course that would be tough! She was so nurturing. She always watched out for him. Protecting him. Playing with him. One minute, off with her medium-size friends—the next moment joining him in a secret game or plan. Taking time out of her group to go over and check up on Will—push him in the baby swing, slide together down a sand hill. She loved him enormously. She orbited around him, like a moon around a planet, circling and observing, zooming in close, then off to bigger-kid play.

I missed it. By accident, I completely bypassed her reality.

I let her walk into a minefield and get blown to bits. I should have prepared her, talked, shared and anticipated her pain. How moronic could I be??!! Such an error.

I see how watchful and careful I must be. Each day I need to give them a pattern. We must speak of Will, and sing his song. In addition to whatever Grandma, Aunt, or any friends do, I *myself* need to repeat certain things over and over for them. When I do, I reassure them of my love for them and him—reiterate our joint loss. I must model for them what to say and what we can do: Here's how we remember his sweetness—Wasn't he funny when he hid your toys there?—We can laugh at Will, even if he isn't right here right now. Also, we can be quiet and sad and still. *However you feel or act* is just fine. I must show them and think ahead for them.

I feel breathless, bewildered at my own stupidity. I'm trying so hard. I failed to recognize what that park playtime symbolizes for Catherine. Please, don't let me miss too many signs, Lord. Please help me keep my wits about me, be insightful.

For their sake, Jesus, for the sake of my little ones, have mercy.

DAY Thirteen

JUNE 14

I have had no time of quiet in this house. The outpouring of love and kind deeds has swallowed us whole. I am grateful for these "hands and feet of God." Christian brothers and sisters who ran to the airport at any hour, day or night; they are so giving. The dear ones who organized meals for us. The businessman friend who is developing a memorial foundation. So many have cried with us.

But what I want more than anything right now is to be given time alone. Time in the quiet.

One friend offered Bob and me her family's cabin two hours away, near a national park. Bob took me there for two days. Bob's sister stayed with our kids so we were free to go.

Alone. Finally. We walked through tall, quiet, old trees, Bob on one path, I on another. Parallel, not able to be together. Relief. Solitude. Peace.

I miss William terribly—the size of the pain is like the size of terror. But no one gives me any time to remember. I want to think about him, to remind myself he was not a myth, not a

Remember me when I am gone away,
Gone far away into the silent land;
When you can no more hold me by the hand,
Nor I half turn to go, yet turning stay.
Remember me when no more day by day,
You tell me of our future that you plann'd:
Only remember me; you understand
It will be late to counsel then or pray.
Yet if you should forget me for a while
And afterwards remember, do not grieve:
For if the darkness and corruption leave
A vestige of the thoughts that once I had,
Better by far you should forget and smile
Than that you should remember and be sad.

CHRISTINA ROSSETTI

pretend being. He really lived. He really was solid and real. When I am given the space, then I can weep, and call out to him, and to God. Then I feel once more like a real person, myself. The rest of the time I am a robot—going about the house mechanically, devoid of feelings or interest. It's all a fake. There's no reality. I put on an act. And I don't believe he's dead. Too busy.

So please, all of you caring hearts, won't you leave me alone? Just for a time? I need you, but now it's all too noisy, too hectic. I need some everyday-ness to reappear. Some "normalcy."

Oh, please, everyone, go away.

He gives his sunlight to
both the evil and the
good, and he sends rain
on the just and on the
unjust, too.

MATTHEW 5:45

DAY Fourteen

JUNE 15

Two weeks. It's midafternoon. I moved people around so that the computer room is now available; now it will be free anytime I want it, day or night. I am afraid I hurt my sister-in-law's feelings by putting her in the children's room. And my own sister was shifted to a friend's home nearby. But I had to do it. Right now I have to set things up in a way to help me think and breathe—just to survive. Sometimes the pain is so physical; it builds up in my throat and chest, and I feel like I have a steel box inside. Clamping tight on my lungs, my neck.

Family and friends, forgive me when you understand, later; people I love, forgive. I do only what I must—I cannot let anything or anyone get in the way. Somehow each day I will find growth, I will find good, I will find God. I will not waste this terribly expensive pain; I will let no one and nothing interfere. No matter if they misunderstand. I will make *life* and *peace* of what God is giving me. He will do it. He will enable it to be so. Nothing matters but this: Let me not rebel. *Let me not rebel.* Dear God, don't let me become a rebel. Help me accept what You give.

The rain falls on the just and unjust alike.[1] I do not expect only good things to happen to me. My friend Sally Rumsey wrote a song for Will and sang it at the memorial service. Unbelievable. It could only have come from the Holy Spirit, because it said what I could not yet verbalize—what my heart could not yet say:

> *Life is a gift we've received*
> *So let us live in the fullness of each day*
> *Love is a gift we can share;*
> *Our hearts were made to be given away.*
> *We never know what tomorrow may bring,*
> *So let us live today with all the joy and laughter we can find,*
> *And with our faith in the grace of the Lord—*
> *We can receive all He has to give.*
>
> *Children are a gift from the Lord;*
> *Through them He shows us how He wants us to live.*
> *Their simple faith and their trust*
> *Remind us of*
> *The gentle love that the Lord wants to give . . .*
> *We never know what tomorrow may bring . . . we can*
> *. . . Receive all He has to give.*

That is it. That last line tells the work I have to do now: Learn to receive this terrible thing. I've spent my whole life building up a relationship with God, a love and a trust in Him. That does not change in one day, one week, one month. *He does not change.*

So far I am not asking why. In fact, I am asking *why not.* Business friends kindly asked us to dinner. They cried with us—R. J. is an unusually warm and loving person. He said, "This is such an awful tragedy—and to happen to *you*—you are such *good* people—I just can't understand why it happened to you." I said to him that I believe God both *gives* good and *allows* bad things to come. He doesn't give Christians special "leave of absence" from everyday human life and bad stuff.

God has given me great blessings. Will He not also allow some pain, and some grief? Why *not* me? It happens to everyone the world over—death comes to all. I consider myself part of the cloth, the entire fabric of life: mothers, parents—the whole.

But what a nasty path I am now sharing with these others, nameless and faceless people who, like me, have touched death skin to skin. Who are they, the people who have survived this? Let me know them. People from times past who have suffered this loss and kept their faith strong, kept their lives useful.

I do not ask why. But I am asking how.

How, Lord? *How* will You make good of this? What economy can transform this kind of pain? A power I do not yet know.

And into what will it be changed?

How, where, what good will it be? How will it develop? That's my question. I find myself saying it over and over. *How????* How will I live through this day? this hour? Lord Jesus—You who suffered all can do all. I believe final good might be possible—in You. I choose You—I trust You. But the loss, the pain—its sheer size is so great.

How? Over and over, I end up with the same words. Help me, Lord. Jesus, have mercy.

Help me.

Sorrow is one of the things that are lent, not given.
A thing that is lent may be taken away;
a thing that is given is not taken away.
Joy is given;
sorrow is lent.

We are not our own,
we are bought with a price . . .

[Our sorrow] is lent us for just a little while
that we may use it for eternal purposes.
Then it will be taken away

and everlasting joy will be
our Father's gift
to us,
and the Lord God will wipe away all tears
from off all faces.

AMY CARMICHAEL, *Edges of His Ways*

DAY Sixteen

JUNE 17

I look at this journal so far, and it's almost funny. At one point I really want and need people. An instant later, I want to be alone. Is this normal? Am I a bit crazy? Back and forth. Irritable. Fickle.

Probably both needs are normal, true. If I were alone all the time, I would get obsessed with the pain, the loss. Crazed. When I am around people, I am pulled out of this great sadness, into the outer world others inhabit. I need their laughter, as counterpoint to grief. Like breathing in, and suffering. Then breathing out, and finding (briefly) relief.

And I *need* to cry. The people who irritate me the most are the ones who say, "Be strong." Implicit in this phrase I feel them saying, "Don't cry. Don't give way to your grief. If you must, then cry only a little. Don't show your sorrow. Hide your pain. . . ." What a stupid thing to say. How infantile. As if emotions ought to be stifled and suppressed—for *their* peace of mind?

The people I most appreciate say things like, "Be patient.

Give yourself time and space. Wait on God." Take time to come to grips with this, they imply. Give yourself and others room to maneuver through this experience—be patient. That makes sense to me: God is working out His plan and pattern. Not everything is visible just now. I can't see the whole. Another excellent phrase a good friend wrote was: "I can't understand this. But we love you. We are really heartbroken *with* you." That brings comfort.

Pastor Jerry said that there is such a thing as "grief work." Things to do, steps we should not avoid. Face up, walk through. He said that the work of grief is remembering. He said we should keep *talking* and *talking* about Will to each other and keep the happy memories alive. Eventually, he said, the bitter sting will be replaced by a long deep sadness, without the evil aftertaste. And finally joy—happy recollections only.

A healthy, remembering kind of love. One that lets go, accepts, and yet does not evade the reality of the loss.

Many different things keep me sane—give me comfort. Some have fancy Christian doctrine names, like *sovereignty*. But the simple words express it best: I believe God kept His hand of control over every detail. It is as if God said: *Yes, this child will die. But only in a specific manner. It will not be like that or that. I will allow only this way, this time. I will place My hedge around My children. I will dictate the circumstances surrounding this death. Here are the boundaries. This far, and no further. Death will come, but on My terms. These are My children.*

At least three times—probably more—specific things have happened to remind me that God is there. (Small, rustling, fresh wind entering my deep stillness.) I will wake up in the morning, dreading the day. Lying there wishing to hear, just one more time, the happy, birdlike baby patter from the crib.

And some specific heart query—*hunger*—will stretch itself out toward heaven. And in a miraculous way, each time, heaven hears my heart's cry.

One day my thought was, *Oh, Jesus, please give Baby Will a big kid to chase, to love and mimic, to trail along after. How does a toddler feel in heaven?*

Jesus—hear me! He's just a little one. Surely You give him people his *size* . . . ?

Later that day I received a special phone call from Aunt Marion—not a "real" relation but Mom's best friend as a child, my mentor throughout difficult college days. With tearful voice, yet with awe, she told me that her grandson died five years ago. On the *exact* day, June 1.

Now I know. Jake Auwerda—that's William's friend. Jake is there with Will, playing, carrying, and loving my baby. Tickling him. Sitting on him. Showing him a ball and bat. (How Will was beginning to love balls and bats! He never was a stuffed-animal kind of child.) Now I know. You gave him a stand-in big brother. Not some nameless, faceless seraphim (forgive me, angelic beings)! A real-life, rough-and-tumble, fun and happy, sturdy *boy*. I know his family. I know his name. That brings comfort.

Another day, I woke with panic, saying to myself, *How can I help Catherine? What can ease her suffering? How can I lessen the pain in Bobby's heart?* Hours later, a former neighbor came by with a manila envelope in hand. She had photocopied five or six short articles on children and grief.

I cannot concentrate very well. A book seems overwhelming, even to me, a bookworm who devours on vacation two books daily. So these pithy magazine articles—pages—were an exact response to my heart's cry.

God, You are hearing me, lonely speck of dust that I am. You hear my voice. I thank You.

Third incident (in the first ten days): My day to swim. I was dreading the renewed pool activity. I knew it was only a matter of time. Last summer, the children spent *all* their time in the pool. This year, so far, we had only gone swimming during Will's naptime. But as the weather had gotten warmer, I knew there would be the all-day-swim type of days ahead. Summertime.

The pool was only the vehicle of death—not some monster, not a death trap. We would be returning to a normal family life with pool.

I decided—I needed—to be the first one in, relatively soon, so that later I could focus on Bobby and Catherine and any comments or fears or strangeness they might feel. And I wanted to swim alone. No one intruding.

Or so I thought.

When the day actually came, I had a sinking in my stomach. I arranged for the kids to play at friends' houses. I was getting ready to dive into the pool, but strong, churning emotions held me back. My heart was so heavy—almost afraid! What was the matter with me? This water was my son's death. *But it is only water,* I thought.

The doorbell rang. Midafternoon. Marilyn, whose husband died just two years ago, arrived early to deliver a hot meal for our supper. She understood, and was a quiet presence, just there. She sat, and I swam. I got past that hurdle, and the children now swim daily, having fun.

Until the actual moment of preparing to dive in the water, I did not know my need. I couldn't—wouldn't be able to do it. I felt too mixed up, too jumbled up emotionally. God prepared someone to come and stay with me, beside me—when I did not anticipate my heart's fears.

Little things. A nonbeliever might say coincidental. I give the glory to God and say (what comfort this brings) He is listening to me. The Creator of all, Light of lights, Power over all powers, listens to my voiceless cries. He is a personal God. He cares for the little things. Small, fragile people.

"I forget appointments, plane arrival and departure times, who signed up to bring dinner, who brought food yesterday. . . . And I am beginning to forget my own precious baby. Is this shock? What's going on?"

DAY Twenty

JUNE 21

Tomorrow is three weeks. Oh, Lord, how can it be? Surely it is a year, a decade. The minutes drip endlessly, slowly, like a faucet, so irritating. Each one feels like a day. It seems like a year when it's only one hour.

I can't concentrate or retain anything—everyday details elude me. I forget appointments, plane arrival and departure times, who signed up to bring dinner, who brought food yesterday. Where those flowers came from. Was there a phone message? What time are we supposed to be where? (Does it matter?)

And I am beginning to forget my own precious baby. Some little particular details. I can't bring it all to mind instantly, right now. Is this shock? What's going on?

God, how can You be so cruel? How can You allow me to begin to forget? The first few days, every time I put a teacup down, I said quietly to myself, "I could not place this cup here if Will were alive." Little busy fingers. Hands never still, always reaching up to the kitchen counter, the bookshelves, the tables.

Stretching over to tangle the big people things, yearning to participate in the big kids' world.

Getting so tall, getting so big. Able to push the kitchen chairs up to the table and climb up onto the table. Upend the sugar bowl, cereal box, any goodies left there by mistake. I used to call him "Kitten-fingers." His clever fingers reminded me of baby animals' claws—their nails are razor sharp. Often a kitten catches a thread of your sweater and pulls a huge snag. That was Baby Will. He could swipe at your glass of water, and if one solitary finger caught hold, you were wet all over! Clever little guy. Active. Nimble hands. So quick, he was frustrating—and messy—and endlessly cute.

Already I put things down where I never allowed them before. If he is not here, there is no need to worry about that stack of papers, this pile of photos. No one will push them over into disarray, and greater accessibility, on the floor. Big-kid special art projects will not be harmed by sticky fingerprints—precious hands of Baby Will. Oh, God, I miss that mess. I miss the frustration. I hate the smoothness of every day. How I hate myself for having an easy time cleaning the house. How I hate errands being so simple and arms being free to carry groceries and bags. How I hate it all! I would trade every single convenience

> *for*
>> *just*
>>> *one*
>>>> *more*
>>>>> *time*

one single hour, one tiny *moment,* of frustration or discomfort or annoyance or even downright disobedience of those busy, endlessly active little precious, priceless hands and feet. Jesus,

Jesus, look on my tears and remember me. Don't forget me in my pain! Don't—don't let me forget my baby's ways.

Oh, can I not hold him one more time? Oh, can I not give him one, just one, small hug? Oh, how could one small cuddle upset the entire balance of Your universe!? Is it really all so precariously intertwined? Jesus, Jesus, be reasonable. Must the whole thing be so utterly absolute? Must he be completely *not mine* anymore? Jesus, Jesus, do not forget me now.

"Love is undying, and life is unending, and the boundary of this mortal life is but a horizon, and a horizon is nothing save the limit of our sight."

DAY Twenty-Two

JUNE 23

A missionary friend sent this prayer (emphasis mine):

> We give them back to You, O Lord, who first gave them
> to us; yet as You did not lose them giving, so we do not
> lose them by their return, *for what is Yours is ours* also if we
> belong to You. Love is undying, and life is unending, and
> the boundary of this mortal life is but a horizon, and a
> horizon is nothing save the *limit of our sight.* Lift us up,
> strong Son of God, that we may see further. Cleanse our
> eyes that we may see clearly . . . and while You prepare a
> place for us, *prepare us* also for that happy place, that we
> may be with You, and with those we love, forevermore.
> Amen.
>
> —*Bede Jarrett, O. P.*

"I was telling Mom today how comforting the friends are who acknowledge the reality of what is happening. People who do not belittle our situation—or compare it."

DAY Twenty-Five

JUNE 26

Mom and Dad are here: missionaries from Africa; not simple to come. Not inexpensive, either. They immediately wanted to be here with us. But they were not sure how and if it could all be arranged. Missionaries receive fixed incomes, usually—and often their allowance is made up of $10 gifts from elderly Christian widows on pensions. Sweet ladies who give sacrificially, selflessly. My parents take great care of the money given to them—they feel a real burden to manage it well. Could they justify a large outlay solely for the succor of their grown child, far away, come for their "convenience," in a sense? Is this a luxury or a necessity? They *wanted* to come right away, but should they? And anyway, did they have enough funds in their travel account?

As they were struggling and praying questions like these, one of our churches (where my family has a relationship of several generations) came forward. "Please come and be with your children—here's the necessary money!" Unreal. That is how the church of Jesus is supposed to be.

I was telling Mom today how comforting the friends are who acknowledge the reality of what is happening. That brings a kind of relief from pain. People who do not belittle our situation—or compare it: "I knew a family whose baby died in a . . ." Or contrast: "I lost my dear puppy dog last year . . ." This diminishes the uniqueness of our pain, our sorrow.

I hate the ones who say (sugary-sweet), "God needed another little angel!" It is so superficial and bankrupt—their view of a grasping, manipulative god. As if God is needy. As if God is jealous and stingy about our joys, our treasures. Does He begrudge us our small happinesses? Never. He cries with us. And smiles with us.

The problem is their concept of God—how He acts, who He is. And their view of heaven. Harps and white-winged beings with haloed heads—streets of tinfoil. Pathetic. Shallow—sacrilegious religiosity. A veneer of belief over a self-controlled life and "faith."

I value the friends who write in their cards, "When we heard the news, our eyes filled with tears. We weep for you. There's nothing to say. Except we love you, and we are praying. Hold on to God—surely He will help you through even this." That's a useful thing to say—that has solidity, comfort.

Their attitude is clear. It shows several important characteristics. First, an attempt to empathize: "I'm trying to walk in your shoes just now, to imagine it's me, and even *thinking* of the possibility makes me cry out in pain!"

Second, it shows faith. Their statements validate the spiritual world, the unseen, invisible things. Eternity. Life after death. "Eternal truths have not shifted, even though what you are experiencing is huge, overwhelming, right now. There are absolutes that you can count on: gravity is still gravity, God is still

God. He still cares for you. This tragedy does not cancel out the facts: He is able to help, to succor you. We don't know what to do. But God can reach you, so we are praying. In this terrible time, reach out to Jesus, dear one." These friends lend me words of faith in my darkness. Thoughtful, kind statements of God's character, God's *being*.

Finally, their words show gentleness. Sensitivity. Sensibility. "We *feel* for you in your suffering. We don't have pat answers; we have emotions that vibrate in response to your situation. We are not trying to solve and erase your pain. We haven't discovered a formula to dry up your tears." (Many people send formulas: rote phrases rather than thought-out words for your hurt. Smart little ditties, cute and pretty. No sense, no sensibility. *Augh!*) The wise friends say, "We can't let one more day go by without sending you a note to say this, just this: We really, really care. We are so very sorry this has happened."

More than once . . . we were brought face to face
with the old, old problem of pain. . . .
Some [explanations] were too simple;
some were too complex.
Either way
they left us where we were. . . .

Our Father Himself will solve
the problem [of pain]
in the day of which it is written,
And God shall wipe away
all tears from their eyes.

When we are in the fierce grip of pain,
or when our soul cleaveth unto the dust
in the dull heaviness
that follows pain,
we care not at all
about solving a problem,

all we want is strength to come through
unsubdued.
This was what we asked for.

AMY CARMICHAEL, *Though the Mountains Shake*

DAY Twenty-Nine

JUNE 30

A subject I am pondering these days is this: It seems like people are punished for loving more. That makes me angry. I feel like I will suffer more because I loved him so deeply. If I'd loved him less, I'd hurt less now.

My children made me realize this. Unlike other families I've seen, we have taught our children to love one another, to be respectful, even when angry or provoked. I am not saying they never disagree or fight. That'd be lying. They have bad moments, of course. But they are not allowed to say deeply hurtful and personally rude remarks: not to each other, not to me. I've taught my kids to stay away from belittling words, and express their anger and frustration clearly without hurtful slang. Then there is reconciliation—they hug and state verbally their forgiveness. "You're my sister—I love you. You are a friend, I'm sorry. Let's go play." Good words in the mouths of children.

As a result, they have real affection for each other—hug and walk hand in hand from time to time. Genuine enjoyment. All three had this.

So I feel angry that my kids, who worked to develop this, who were knit together in a healthy family way, are now torn apart. They feel it. They ache with it. They miss him. He was a charming and delightful player in their daily life games. He was the clever one who took their toys—denuded the flower bushes—hid their Duplos and Legos. They were proud of him. He was the one they looked out for, laughed at, tickled, and finally sat on when they could no longer control his behavior (he was getting so big and strong).

So it seems like they will suffer more deeply because they loved more deeply. That's not fair. If this is true, it's an unjust penalty for good behavior.

I know—I choose again to know—that the facts of eternity do not change. God does not send pain to punish bad behavior; He is not a malicious God. He is good. So my reasoning must be wrong somewhere.

Years ago I studied *The Divine Comedy* by Dante and learned that faith is a choice. We move our volition toward *belief* over *disbelief.* Faith must be based on good, solid, common sense—yes. But in the end, there's a gap where rationality ends. A gulf at the end of human thought and reason. You throw yourself across—you choose to leap that last gap. (You are enabled to get across.) It's something—Someone—you throw yourself into, and obey, and hear the quiet Voice.

Help me, You who enclose all mysteries—help me to see how this wonderful family love will bear some fruit, now that we are splintered with pain.

There's my old *how* question again. (I said that was my word!) How can his absence bring wholeness to us? Strange mystery. Paradox? O Holder of my smallest boy, *how?*

BOOK TWO

The Center
of Darkness

Do not go gentle into that good night . . .
Rage, rage against the dying of the light.

DYLAN THOMAS

DAY Thirty-One

JULY 2

Month two has begun.

Bob is not talking as much now, and I'm a bit worried about him. He has begun to bury himself in the insatiable demands of work. I imagine the finiteness is comforting, but his long hours and lack of talking frustrate me. I hate what the executive world demands of a man, of his family. It's too much.

He says he still stops, almost daily, and cries before work. He says he pulls over at one particularly beautiful place on the highway and bawls. Why can't he cry here at home? Why can't he *tell me* what he is thinking and feeling?! I only find out when I yell at him and press him to the wall, accusing him of not caring, not feeling. Only then does he confess his daily crying place. Only then will he acknowledge that he likes the escape of work. This house is a house of death to him.

In the beginning, he told me he had panic attacks at work. He'd work for several hours, and then, overcome with fear and anxiety, he'd have to leave—go for a long walk—before continuing that day. He has fewer now, he says.

The children and I are OK—we spend long periods talking of Will, remembering. Then we'll spend an afternoon barely mentioning his name. (We are all conscious of his absence, just busy with regular things.) A grief/psych book I am reading says there's an important balance between laughing and crying. Not that you can measure and increase or decrease according to a standard amount. (You scored high on mental health, Mrs. Faber . . . I'm sorry, you scored low . . .) But that each person-ality will develop its own correct amount—grief is so individ-ual. This book only says *both* should occur.

My parents left. Before they went, the children and I had a balloon ceremony. Each of us drew a picture or wrote a message for Will. Then we each chose a special Will helium balloon at the store. We went to a large open park—and released the balloons with the message/drawings attached to them. Mom and Dad came along to give supportive pres-ence. Quiet, prayerful.

Up, up they went. Smaller, smaller. Three balloons floating slowly up to God.

Tears. Laughter. I told Bobby, as we sobbed, "We watch the balloons and say, *'There* they go, good-bye, good-bye.' But, Bobby, at the other end, someone is saying 'Hello, hello!' In heaven Will was greeted warmly: 'We waited for you. We see you now. Hello! Welcome!' Bobby, they were happy to hold him, hug him there. They love him. Baby Will is there now." Thank God, it's not pretend. He's there.

> I am standing on the seashore. A ship spreads her white sails to the morning breeze and starts for the ocean. I stand watching her until she fades on the horizon, and someone at my side says, "She is gone."

Gone where? The loss of sight is in me, not in her. Just at the moment when someone says, "She is gone," there are others who are watching her coming. Other voices take up the glad shout, "Here she comes," and that is *dying*.

—*Henry Scott Holland*

"Sometimes the pressure inside builds up and gets so great, I feel I am going to explode. That's why I am so irritated and angry with my children, I think. I haven't had enough time to cry, to be alone, to be quiet."

DAY Thirty-Three

JULY 4

My throat keeps turning to steel, a metal box. Sometimes I can hardly breathe, it hurts so much. These past weeks, one friend from church has helped me in an unusual way—a peculiar way, I guess. She has taken me for "screaming rides" in the car. I never would have thought something like that helpful before losing Will.

Driving in the far lane, windows down, loud music playing—she tells me to call out to God, loudly. Cry. Call out to Will. I shout in a huge voice, I plead, I beg, I argue. The relief is tangible in my body. Physical release. Those car rides draw floods of tears, healing, crying.

Sometimes the pressure inside builds up and gets so great, I feel I am going to explode. That's why I am so irritated and angry with my children, I think. I haven't had enough time to cry, to be alone, to be quiet.

Why does the tension from tears unspent settle in my shoulders, my neck, my throat? Why can't I find release in a less dramatic way? I don't know and I don't care. All I know is those screams are real, and they tell the truth that my tears *would* tell if they weren't trapped.

Those screams turn to calls, those calls turn to tears, and those tears are answered. Every time. I know I am answered.

DAY Thirty-Eight

JULY 9

Well, I have no idea if I'm on schedule or not in my grief process. I'm full of anger today, full of sadness, full of anguish.

Oh, God, must You be so unrelenting? Must death be a one-way street? Is it completely permanent? It feels like You have no mercy. The only thing I desire is reversal, pardon. A change of heart, a change of purpose/plan. But perhaps I could not have any shade of adjustment without damaging the whole picture of Your giving for today.

It's hard to believe that You are that iron-formed, God. And yet in other circumstances, I want You to be that immovable, that unchangeable. Unaffected by my shilly-shallying. Not dented by my questions. In a sense, impervious to my tossing about, stormy times, wavering wimpiness.

When I am able to breathe and am not drowning in pain, I rest in that bigness. I lean back on God's solid size. But this morning I fell out of Him and into the pit. Oh, hook me back, Jesus! Grab onto me—don't let me slide all the way to the bottom. I must go there. But help me walk down one step at a time, into that valley. Not slither, zoom, drown. I was thinking the other day that death isn't really a valley. What was David saying in the Psalms? "Yea, though I walk through the valley of the shadow of death . . ."[2] For me, it's a granite mountain, snow covered: an incline, slippery, icy, jagged. You can't get a firm hold on anything. Your hands get cut on sharp rock bits; you feel powerless against this huge, uncaring mass. You must go on, but you can only go slowly. You slip a lot. But you must keep on. I stumble forward on bleeding knees.

Day Forty

JULY 11

Outline of my feelings during the first six weeks:

First week: Sick, knees buckling all day, sleepless. Physically incapable of performing routines. Constant sensation of weakness.

Ten days: No realization of facts. The buffer surrounded us completely—meals, visitors, arrivals, departures, conversation, travel of family and friends all happened without any effort on our part. Inner silence and waiting, in a cocoon. (Waiting for *what?* I don't know.)

Twenty days: Shafts of pain beginning to penetrate cocoon. Awful, but bearable because arrows of pain are separated by distractions and kind, fun friends. At this point, it was like we were covered by a sieve (small holes = sharp times of grief separated by flat dullness/no holes). Reality touched us needle-like, but mostly we were protected. Like the weird cap a woman wears at a beauty salon when she gets her hair colored or highlighted: The hat covers her entire scalp—looks like hair is totally shielded. Hardly visible, there are minute holes in this cap. The stylist pulls a few threads of hair through each tiny hole to receive the harsh chemicals. That was how it felt: bits of the awful truth seeping into my mind and heart, jabbing insistently at times, but not the full brunt of loss and death. Sections of great pain, sections of laughter and "normalcy."

Forty days: Black, bleak, dark, angry. Losing a sense of God's presence and care. Hard to believe He is here with me now.

DAY Forty-One

JULY 12

Well, this is the dark slope. Very little light here now. What there is, I've placed there myself: small tapers, lit and set down with words of faith from a dry, hot brain.

God is good (I tell myself). That is one of those fundamental facts. As I am crying, I say to the children, "William is not coming back." Inside I am screaming out, "Don't go . . . don't go . . . don't go!" as if I have some control. As if I have some say. As if my plea can affect the outcome, when the obscene reality is that everything is all over. He is gone, completely, absolutely, irrevocably.

Here and now, there's a vast emptiness, with piercing anguish expanding, growing, exploding in my heart. Here and now there's only tears, cries, more tears that flow, never stopping. How pitiful that only days ago I was laughing and able to be distracted by a book, a movie (going for Bob's sake, for the sake of friends who invite us). Now is only darkness and only silence.

God? Is He here? I keep telling myself, "He cries *with* me."

Sometimes we wake feeling down,
and we feel like that all day long
for no reason
that we can discover—only it is so.

It is useless to try to feel different;
trying does not touch feelings.

It is useless to argue with oneself;
feelings elude arguments.

Be patient—
feelings are like the mists that cover the mountains
in misty weather.
The mists pass;
the mountains abide.

Turn to your Father,
tell Him you know that He loves you
whether you feel it or not,
and that you know that He is with you
whether you feel His presence or not. . . .

Ask the Holy Spirit to bring some saying of His to your
    mind
that has helped you in the past.
[A] saying wherein He has caused us to trust.

The mists pass;
the mountains abide.

AMY CARMICHAEL, *Edges of His Ways*

Otherwise I would lash out at God right now. I would scream in bitterness, if I did not *say,* with no sense of its trueness, "He sees the sparrow. He sees me now."

Just the thought, just the saying, in complete disbelief brings a thin ray of hope. God, help me. God who counts the penny-priced birds, hear me.

There is no refuge in my world. No place to go. No location allows surcease from pain.

Church is strange: I carry no diaper bag there. (It's agony and real suffering to look at his baby bag. He loved to unpack it and examine each item. He was bold and pushy over his bag. He considered it *his* territory—indisputable! He knew no one would argue.)

Grocery stores are strange: Our food-buying list has changed. Will was a steady eater—not gluttonous, but with a large and consistent appetite. Now we do not require as much food, nor the huge amount of milk we needed for his daily bottles and cups.

Driving in the car is the worst: The hollow place where his car seat went screams at me daily.

Home is strange: There is no place empty of this emptiness. In every area we see and feel the lack of him. Every day.

The worst thing people do now is ignore the fact that he is gone. They're in a quandary, my friend Diana said. They don't want to mention his name, because they don't want to disturb me, make me cry, if I'm having a happy moment. The dilemma is whether to interrupt "one happy moment," to press the grief in my face again, or to take the easy way out and say nothing of my situation. But if people don't acknowledge his absence, it feels like they are idiots or completely uncaring. What people forget is that you *never* forget. The grief is *always* in your face, *always* there. It's far better for them to speak and show they care.

I went to Communion last night. Everyone asked how we were, in a hushed, intense way. (Like, "You can tell *me*. You can share your pain with *me*. Let me be the confidante.") There? In a public place? In front of lots of people? Say what I really feel?

But no one said his name. No one asks, "What are you remembering about William today? Which photo of him are you carrying with you—can I see it?" I need that. I need to hear his name.

DAY Forty-Three

JULY 14

"His eye is on the sparrow, and I know He watches me." I've been losing that sense, that belief. You are restoring this for me, God. Suffering and only Son: Watcher of Will. Watcher of sparrows. Watcher of me. Thank You.

I am only one leaf in the whole forest, a tiny blade of grass on the lawn of today. Withering. Drying. Fading. Dying. Yet You know my *name*. You call me by name. You called Will by name.

The books I am reading are a massive help. These past five days I have felt at the end of my tether. Ready to scream all the time. Having an inner breakdown—spiritually depleted—finished. Coming apart, turning inside out: up is down, and down is up? Cold, dry, tearless. No expression of grief, just aggravation, anger. My irritation level has been so high with Bobby and Catherine. I have no patience. The house overwhelms me. Too many chores and not enough time or energy. At the best of times, I am a slow worker. This week, useless. I lost my heart's peace this week.

But a book by Joe Bayly *(The Last Thing We Talk About)* and another one by Elisabeth Elliot *(A Path Through Suffering)* have redirected my feelings and renewed my belief and sense of God's presence. Although she is sometimes a bit fierce, Elisabeth Elliot is, and has been for years, a hero of mine. She was a missionary to savage tribes in Ecuador when her husband, Jim, was martyred. Later, her second husband died of cancer. Yet she never whimpers; she never says God is unfair. I buy everything she writes. I chew, swallow, digest, and am deeply nourished by her. I thank God for her!

Joe Bayly was a church friend of my family. His writings carry deep credibility: He lost three sons at various ages—one to leukemia, one in a climbing accident, and one as an infant. A kind man, a warm man, he was a brilliant communicator, leading nonconforming, lively debates in our Sunday school classes. Yet his intelligence was secondary to his deeply compassionate heart. In his books, he gathered quotes from incredible sources. One German theologian said:

> Only He who inflicts the wounds and permits them is able also to heal them. No one else. Illusions about death cannot do this; neither can hushed silence on the subject. Even the atheistic method of easy dying . . . only teaches how to bleed to death without looking. . . . No, God alone can heal the wound. . . . I am one whose history with God cannot stop, since I am called by my name and I am the friend of Jesus. The Resurrected One is victorious and I stand within His sphere of power. . . . It is not . . . something supposedly immortal within me that brings me through. . . . [He] can no more abandon me

on the other side than He could let me out of His hand here on this side of the grave.[3]

Joe Bayly also said that death makes us assess the meaning and worth of *life.* "When you accept the fact of death, you are freed to live."[4] Also helpful is his reminder that one hundred out of one hundred people die. One hundred percent.

Knowing that helps, I guess, because if it happens to *everyone,* you are not being persecuted. Death is no respecter of persons. It's universal, and we are not being singled out for some solitary punishment. Ahead of everyone on the face of the earth, sometime, is death. Sooner or later. Eighteenth-century philosopher Voltaire said that "we begin to die as soon as we are born."

One of Joe's kids died of leukemia. I really relate to his conclusion: He believed that his son was totally in God's hands.

> Shortly after our five-year-old died of leukemia, someone asked me how I'd feel if a cure for leukemia were then discovered. My answer was that I'd be thankful, but it would be irrelevant to the death of my son. God determined to take him to His home at the age of five; the means was incidental.[5]

That's exactly how I feel. The *means,* William's drowning in our pool, was incidental. It was one of many ways to die. If God is sovereign, these phrases are not merely fatalistic. They present actual reality. God counted the days of Will's life—the hairs on his head. The breaths in his body. The number was finished. Will lived 100 percent—*one hundred percent*—of his life. He was complete.

I've been losing my grip on that other reality, the unseen Reality. I'm not sure why. Maybe it's just the battle of daily living—someone said, "It's the dailiness of life that I don't like." Perhaps it's the people around me. I much prefer to be alone these days. Good writers are the best kind of people to have around; these books really helped me get focused again. Amy Carmichael is another outstanding person. (Was!) Her poems turn me to Jesus.

Simple, childlike songs also pierce my disbelief. My guardian from boarding-school days in Kenya, Nan Green, sent me the words to an old, familiar hymn: "I must tell Jesus all of my trials. I cannot bear these burdens alone. In my despair, He'll comfort and cheer me. Jesus will help me—*Jesus alone.*"[6]

DAY Forty-Five

- -

JULY 16

After reading more on bereavement and coping with death, notably the secular press and psychologists, I realize why so many people who came to my door that first week said, "Be strong!" A lot of parents lose their ability to live a normal life following the loss of a child. They freak out. I understand this reaction—grief at times swamps you. Constantly, I turn away from the pain and accept the next thing, the task that must be done next. So far, I haven't gotten to where I can't cope with routine things. Many folks weren't able to leave the house— panic attacks. They suffered prolonged fear of the outside world. My issues have mostly been *internal*—an inner crisis with coping. Atypically for me, the household things—like doing dishes—are kind of soothing!

My struggle is a war with myself. *Sin*-self. Perhaps self-pity. My fight is spiritual. Emotions deep within. I work to keep my head above water—in the light, not in the darkness. "Facing the sun . . . letting the shadows fall behind." Some dear bereaved ones can't even face going to the store, going out to

Facing the sun and letting the shadows fall behind . . .

My great-aunt RUTH CHURCHILL
on the loss of her only child,
an infant daughter, December 1931

the post office. Don't go to church. Stop attending clubs. Don't step out of the house.

I feel for these suffering people, but it has been different so far for me. The logistics of my life are nearly the same (slightly less running around in the car, maybe). It's my inner listening I'm worried about. I am concerned to hear the voice of Jesus. I cannot face this without hearing His voice. I'd die. I cannot move into the next hour, let alone the next day, alone.

Bob and I are not together in the emotions of this. In the first days after William's death, Bob was the crying, emotional one and I was calm, frozen. He was talkative and hugged people a lot. That was unusually expressive for him. He's the cool, intellectual German type.

As the weeks have passed, things are changing. I've become more emotional; he's become less so (externally, at least). I'm unsure what is happening inside him—is he angry? Is he questioning God? Sometimes I refer to William or the memorial service and get no response. Clearly this is an unwelcome topic. Am I bringing him back into the pain, when he was thinking (briefly) of something else? I guess so.

I struggle to find a time that is acceptable to speak of William. I want to draw close to Bob and share what he is feeling. I want him to know how awful I'm feeling and comfort me. I want to be together.

The worst time of the day is bedtime. I survived one more day with William filling my thoughts, but not my words. I did not mention him obsessively to the kids, just a sprinkle here and there, cheerfully, sadly, however. Trying to live in the present, but acknowledge the past. I let the children determine my pace, the frequency of mentioning his name. I held myself back, in, and watched and listened to them.

Batter my heart, three-personed God; for You
As yet but knock, breathe, shine, and seek to
    mend;
That I may rise and stand, o'erthrow me, and
    bend
Your force to break, blow, burn, and make me
    new.
I, like a usurped town, to another due,
Labor to admit You, but O, to no end;
Reason, Your viceroy in me, me should defend,
But is captived, and proves weak or untrue.
Yet dearly I love You, and would be loved fain,
But am betrothed unto Your enemy.
Divorce me, untie or break that knot again;
Take me to You, imprison me, for I,
Except You enthrall me, never shall be free,
Nor ever chaste, except You ravish me.

JOHN DONNE
(my favorite poet)
Holy Sonnets, #14

My present was deeply tangled in grief, but all day long I set my feelings aside.

When bedtime comes, I want free speech—no more restraints. I'm ready for an orgy of emotion. At times I explode in sorrow. Unluckily for me, however, Bob's excursion into the world of emotional expression is behind him. He's back on target, his focus on business, his energy spent there. He doesn't have the strength or desire for analysis and introspection anymore. Being a good provider seems to take every ounce of him.

I feel bottled up, desperate to talk, needing to cry. He wants only to make love and go to sleep. If I cry, he can't sleep. If I talk, he doesn't want to make love. This is not a good time in our marriage. We need the opposite things. We aren't working well together or helping each other right now.

We are weathering it with a mixture of silence and crying. Some sleepless nights we go out at midnight or early morning, to pace the aisles of those twenty-four-hour grocery stores. We come home, exhausted, and sleep fitfully. It is one of the least together times in our joined lives. We try, but we can't hear each other very well.

Far from Bob, and even farther from William, I feel so lonely. I have to be close to God, or I can't do this. I can't do life.

The important things are very clear, yet I can make myself deaf. Oh, God, let this not be wasted pain. Let this time work in me the work You intended. Let my baby not have died in vain.

Jesus hath many lovers of His heavenly kingdom, but few bearers of His Cross. He hath many seekers of comfort, but few of tribulation. He findeth many companions of His table, but few of His fasting. All desire to rejoice with Him, few are willing to undergo anything for His sake. Many follow Jesus that they may eat of His loaves, but few that they may drink of the cup of His passion.

Many are astonished at His Miracles, few follow after the shame of His Cross. Many love Jesus so long as no adversities happen to them. Many praise Him and bless Him, so long as they receive any comforts from Him. But if Jesus hide Himself and withdraw from them a little while, they fall either into complaining or into too great dejection of mind.

But they who love Jesus for Jesus' sake, and not for any consolation of their own, bless Him in all tribulation and anguish of heart as in the highest consolation. And if He should never give them consolation, nevertheless they would always praise Him and always give Him thanks.

THOMAS À KEMPIS, *The Imitation of Christ*

DAY Forty-Eight

JULY 19

The pool fence was installed today. My church's children's play group is here. I am not bothered for myself—the fence has nothing to do with me or Will. The fact that others must be uncomfortable and insecure matters. I don't want people to consider my place unsafe for them or their children. The fence was expensive, though.

I had not realized F. B. Meyer said that "gold" bit. I heard the quote in a sermon once. Joe Bayly writes:

> I read a comment by F. B. Meyer, that in heaven all earth's values are turned upside down. "What do we count most valuable on earth?" he asked. "Gold. Men live for gold, kill for it. But in heaven gold is so plentiful that they pave the streets with it instead of macadam."[7]

I can see that by this precious baby's death many bad things can be pruned in me—You want to heal me of the sicknesses of this world. I have many infections in my heart and values.

Work Your work in me. May my life be turned upside down as I fix my thoughts on the King of heaven.

As Will does. Will thinks only of Jesus and His glory. Will is completely whole and healed, saying "Holy is the Lamb." He sings to Jesus and works for Jesus, in his little child way. Sometimes, when I sing songs of praise, when the beauty of the music is so intense, I feel I can hear his echo. I can almost join in on the edge of the crowd, always crying, "Holy, holy."

DAY Forty-Nine

JULY 20

Brenda, a friend who lives far away, wrote and asked me to describe Will. How? On a piece of paper, summarize who he was? I appreciate the question (greatly!) but feel frustrated with my effort.

My sweet Wills. Eighteen months of love, joy, surprise, and delight wrapped into a compact bundle. Stocky frame, solid but not fat. He was a quiet child—Maria said a serious boy. (My dear German friend—when I left William with her, he would actually watch me walk away, waving happily. The one he loved.) Catherine is a chatterbox—constant prattle, softly directed at her dolls and toys. Will toddled around humming softly. Speaking little. He was very watchful and clever: alert, questing. He had strong pirate tendencies (thus his nickname and Halloween costume!). He'd steal your goodies of any kind—barrettes, purse, toys, Matchbox cars—and make a quick, but never clean, getaway. He always grabbed too many things, more than he could hold. He'd strew a trail along behind, a bit dribbled here, another piece dropped there, that would lead

Carried by angels—it is all we know
Of how they go;
We heard it long ago.
It is enough; they are not lonely there,
Lost nestlings blown about in fields of air.
The angels carry them; the way, they know.
Our kind Lord told us so.

AMY CARMICHAEL

you clearly to his hideaway. Behind a chair, around the corner, out of sight—the pile of missing goods. His plunder, his booty. At the memorial service Bob said, "Our Pirate, our treasure, is in heaven now. . . . God gave everyone a map . . . the Bible . . . and there's a clear trail to take us there. Follow the treasure map to heaven, to Jesus."

His little hands were square in palm, like his square body. He was unusually easygoing. A third child often is, they say. Baby-sitters and nursery workers at church always commented on his cheerful, straightforward ways. He was physically strong and big; he always tried to keep up with Catherine and Bobby. He had a grip of iron. He'd grab a toy and hold on for dear life—otherwise some big kid might snatch it away! He wanted more than anything to be *big,* to have all the rights and privileges of *bigness* (like the older kids). So he quietly complained when you treated him as "little": putting him in the high chair or car seat, cutting his food into small pieces. No sir! He could handle the big stuff! He took initiative—he was a seeker. He'd push any chair to any table to climb to any height, to find any treasure.

He loved the out-of-doors (Bob is a major nature lover). He preferred real, live animals and scorned stuffed, soft toys. He loved dogs, birds, and squirrels. We have a particularly cheeky black squirrel in the front yard: Will loved to chase him, and call out to him in a friendly voice: Hello ("Heh-doe!"). Bye-bye ("Dye-*dye"*). Among Catherine's dolls he never liked the hard plastic ones, but he'd cuddle the realistic looking ones, play with them. I am an avid gardener and grow different flow-ers; he loved to gather the buds off my bushes, ravish them, oblivious to the damage he was doing. He surely believed his handful of bruised leaves and flowers was just like my bouquets and arrangements—but what a clutter of petals I'd find here and there.

Anything like a ball game was a new and growing passion for him. He dragged a baseball bat around, inside the house and outside. The larger ones weighed almost as much as he did! Sports—big-boy games of any type fascinated him.

One special memory shows both his persistence and final compliance. The sliding door to our courtyard is visible from the kitchen window. William was not supposed to go out for some reason—the mud or his bare feet or whatever. But he saw the door half-open and ran his hand down the opening. With one finger, he outlined the step.

I called out, "No!"

He looked around but could see me nowhere. He lifted his foot to go out.

Again I said, "No, Baby Will."

Amazed, he looked around again trying to figure out where I was. Seeing no one, he prepared to go, but I said no again. Frustrated but obedient, he sat down suddenly, there by the door, and burst into tears.

Like my other two, he was secure and confident, even around new people. He was particularly fond of those smaller than himself—he got a real thrill out of seeing babies. He was sociable and loved toddlers, yes, and big kids. Unusually generous, he'd share the last bite of his last cookie with you without complaint. And he expected the same courtesy of you! Your honeyed toast and cold tea were fair game: one for me, one for you. Your bite? Now mine. Always, always, he'd mutter "Ha-*hot*," with clear consonants, and great disgust, around my hot drinks. Steer clear of that mug of hot stuff.

As I wrote my letter to Brenda, the tears dripped down,

splashing my hands on the computer keyboard. Her questions helped me deeply because in answering her, William came back to life. What a gift sensitive friends are. How I miss my Pirate, my quiet one, my sweet Wills!

"Bob planned for over a year to go and do those wonderful things together. I thought I could manage it, but I was tired and heartsick and sore. Bob and the children were eager to play, and I hated them for their happiness."

DAY Sixty-Five

- -

AUGUST 5

Well. "There and Back Again," as Tolkien—another of my favorite authors—said. Washington, Idaho, and Montana. The universe could not have survived if we had not seen these, I guess. So Bob must have believed. Not I.

We've returned from our first family vacation without Will. I'm sure Bob thinks it was just hunky-dory. Happy campers. Happy trails to you. Just another be-*yoo*-ti-ful sunset, darling. Actually it was more like, "Climb every mountain, ford every stream . . ." Pick up a sample of every example (geologic, that is) in this national park—every rock you can buy. Fill up every minute of every day with meaningless busyness—in a most striking setting.

Bob planned for over a year to go and do those wonderful things together. I thought I could manage it, but I was tired and heartsick and sore. Bob and the children were eager to play, and I hated them for their happiness.

Actually, I was such a consistent grouch that I think my negative, ugly aura penetrated even Bob's (dense?) skull. The children avoided me, and I them, generally. I was happiest separate from all of them. They all irritated me. The kindest thing Bob did was take himself and them away on hike after hike.

I've read every book I can find on bereavement from libraries, bookstores, friends' shelves. Secular or Christian, narrative (personal life stories have helped me the most) or scholarly, you name it, I am trying it. At this moment, I am reading three. I have begun to add some variety to this death diet—absorbing some poetry again and, of course, fiction. Still the main topic for me, of study really, is people who have suffered a loss and survived ("not somehow, but triumphantly" my friends in college used to say). I write: I wrote over forty notes/postcards in our eight days of vacation. I love letters—sending or receiving. This has filled my time—these are things you do in silence and alone.

DAY Sixty-Seven
- -
AUGUST 7

Notable feature of life these days? The awfulness of my
marriage. It's a real pain. We argue over extreme trivia (like
what time we think our host will put the meat on the grill
at the barbeque). We argue with commitment and intensity,
severely. Then when it's over (and I'm the loser again since
Bob is never wrong) we are still, passive. Exhausted, burnt by
our unkindness to each other. Hurting. We don't have the
elasticity we once had. We don't recover as easily from the
nasty inflection in those bickerings. And we are slower to
forgive. It is very difficult.

Every marriage has bad times. Good times. There simply is
no such thing as effortless relationships. This bereavement, our
loss of Will, puts an extra strain on us. We are dealing with it so
differently! I look at photos, keep remembering, speaking with
the children, drawing out their memories of Will, all day long,
every day. To me, it seems like Bob avoids mention of Will. He
fills his days, his hours with work: the world of big business,
success, achievement. Often he (the former misanthrope) loves

to go to parties. While I, the original party animal, can't stand groups of people—more than four makes me tired, cross. I leave and go to an individual, or go somewhere to be alone.

Bob's emotions never were a big topic for conversation. But he has begun, at long last, to speak of his grief. Speaking of the male species, it is no surprise that they don't often say how they feel. Culturally we require them to carry heavy loads and focus on tasks over emotions. We call sensitive men "wimpy." We've trained them into monosyllables: "How was your day?" "Fine."

Now he is trying. Incredible. And twice now, when I was crying, rather than leave the room or ignore my tears, he came and sat by me. He talked with me, and cried with me.

All the books say that the strain a child's death puts on a marriage is enormous. Can't we share this, help each other? Why are we staying so separate; parallel in grief, not touching heart to heart? Why do men and women do it all so differently???

Even the house is falling apart. Owning a home is a pain. There's a leak of some sprinkler-system pipe under the front lawn. The pool is a mess of algae that's clogging the pump. The kitchen drawers have broken handles and can't be opened. It's all a bit much.

DAY Sixty-Eight

AUGUST 8

We just had dinner with friends. Jack is recovering from cancer surgery and now chemotherapy. Life has so many challenges for us to deal with, to learn from. I really pray that we all can grow from this dark stuff, love God more, serve Him better.

I feel so tired sometimes, so very dry and so very old. Listening to good music helps lift me—music of affirmation and hope. Praise songs that remind me of who God is and what He is like. God is good (a fact that cannot change). God loves me (another foundational fact).

Even now, when I am tired and old, repeating the truth can help me at the outset of another day. (When will they all end? When can I see William on that other side?) God, help me face another day. It would be so easy to let go, to give up.

The dailiness of life drags me down, saps my energy. I struggle against myself: my own inertia. My inner self does not want to be alive—not on God's terms, anyway. This awful pain, this Will pain, is a constant reminder, constant call: "Come alive."

*There is something sustaining in the very agitation
that accompanies the first shocks of trouble, just
as an acute pain is often a stimulus and produces
an excitement which is transient strength.*

*It is in the slow, changed life that follows in the
time when sorrow has become stale and has no
longer the emotive intensity that counteracts its
pain, in that time when day follows day in dull
unexpectant sameness, and trial is a dreary
routine—it is then that despair threatens; it is
then that the peremptory hunger of the soul is
felt and eye and ear are strained after some
unlearned secret of our existence, which shall
give to endurance the nature of satisfaction.*

GEORGE ELIOT, *The Mill on the Floss*

To come and be clean in God—come and press closer. Go deeper.

Even as I say this, as the words are forming, there's a struggle. A portion of my heart resists. God, help me to listen to the good, clean voice of Your Spirit. Help me.

BOOK THREE

Passage of Time,
Changes in Grief

A broken altar, Lord, thy servant rears,
Made of a heart, and cemented with tears.

GEORGE HERBERT

DAY One Hundred Forty-Six

OCTOBER 25

One hundred forty-six days. Past the four-month mark. The sheer size of that number is sickening. It seems almost obscene. How can I not have seen Baby Will for this long and survived? How can it be true that I will have a hundred (zillion?) *more* days? I hate the amount of time that has passed. And the amount to come. It disgusts me. God, have mercy.

The summer was far from wonderful—how could it be otherwise? Our family vacation was the lowest point. Now, looking back, I think it's a miracle we made it through. Just to survive our first vacation without our baby was a milestone. You could say we did well, really. We made it and are still, sort of, intact.

Going to New York in August was slightly better. The children and I drove from Chicago, making several stops to see people. We saw little of Bob. He stayed on his treadmill of business travel and long work hours. Our travel and his only intersected briefly in New York City.

Then came September. The first day of school is a family holiday. We make a big event of it: buy special outfits, have favorite breakfasts, take lots of photos. I did everything we usually do— but inside I was furious, screaming in pain. Where was Will? Making family memories, without our baby? A "family" photo without *him?*

We have yet to establish a new routine. There can be no sense of normalcy, really, for a long, long time. How can it be normal for five people to become four?

Poet John Donne said, centuries ago, "No man is an island, entire of itself . . . any man's death diminishes me . . . never send to know for whom the [death] bell tolls; it tolls for thee." When Will died, I died—our family died. We are all changed forever.

We are disabled as a family. The death of a child is an amputation—forced removal of limb, an organ. How does a person learn to live without a leg or an eye? You can. You must. But it is not *normal*. What you move toward is a new definition of *normal*. We say, "She's a quadriplegic—but she taught herself how to write and draw with her mouth." Or "He's lost a leg—he's handicapped." These things become "normal life" for that person. But normal now includes un-normal twisting, crippling, a truncation felt minute after minute, hour after hour. Enormous adjustments are required. How can we keep from bitterness? How can we create joy and gratitude in the new "normal" life?

So we must develop a new family life—fresh patterns will emerge. And I have to get more organized. The family needs it. I am not naturally orderly, nor consistent. I love flexibility and mayhem: creative mess? I always think so. "Set yourself free . . ." says my friend Judith. But children need to know what they can rely on, day by day. They love repetition. They count on it.

We need order, and we need hope.

DAY One Hundred Fifty

OCTOBER 29

It is hard to be realistic about the time frame involved in bereavement. People have no idea how long and how deeply you are affected.

My friends mean well, but they do not always help. No one wants you to feel pain. Everyone wants you to be happy. They are uncomfortable and embarrassed with tears. Yet they also seem confused if you don't show the expressions of grief *they* expect. (I know, I'm hard to please.)

One lady keeps asking, "Is it any better now? Are things a little easier?" I feel like I am a petri dish that she's examining for mold growth. Ah, yes. There's a little blue there; here's a good specimen. Take my temperature, why don't you? I did not have the flu, and I won't "get better." Perhaps she means to say, *How* are you progressing with your sorrow these days? What is it like for you at this time?

Another lady speaks his name gently, and tries to think of hopeful and genuine things to do with the children. One friend often hunts for relevant books at the library or uncovers pertinent magazine articles. She doesn't just *tell* me about these: She goes and gets them and brings them to me. That's friendship. That's practical helping.

Many say nothing at all. Silence is worse than clumsiness. Clumsiness at least makes an attempt. Clumsy people may say the "wrong" words, but you can see their heart is remembering him, remembering William. You can see they think he mattered. You can see they are not forgetting. It hurts to have him forgotten.

People are not prepared for friends in grief. Most lack the life experience. They just don't know what to do. Many simply avoid it, stay away, abdicate. Do they think it's contagious? That's how they treat you. Almost like you have an infectious disease; if they come close to you, perhaps someone *they* love will die.

Death matters. It profoundly affects those around you. At times I've felt like I was walking around in my underwear: exposed, vulnerable. Something private is visible to everyone, and you have no ability to limit your exposure. Everyone sees the curse mark on your head: *Reject. This person's child died! She's different.*

Often if people speak of Will, their words come out jerky and awkward. But at least they tried. Most people—even relatives—never say his name at all. That is the worst. I never hear his precious name, and sometimes in the shower I cry and cry, saying his name over and over. Just to hear the sound, the syllables of that sweet baby name: Will, William, Baby Will, Will. This is one of the hardest things about being so far down this road. Road of grief.

Because people do not know what to say, they fall back on stock phrases, which sound false and insincere due to overuse. I noticed this tendency to say trite words just recently at my grandmother's funeral. Katherine Jones, "Grandma Kay," was a faithful woman, dying at eighty-nine, full of courage and quiet peace. She had a glory and sweetness in the long years she lived.

Most people I spoke with were happy for her, as were we, but so few people I spoke with gave any concession to *our* natural feelings. They only said, "How great for her to be reunited in heaven with those she loved." I say, instead, "How sad and awful for us, because we will miss her. There will not be anyone like her again."

I mourn the loss of my grandmother and her generation. Often the Victorian values are mocked; yet that inner steel is respected. They had a fortitude we lack—backbone. As missionaries in South America my grandparents lived pioneer style: self-denying, serving without financial rewards, enduring discomforts and receiving (in their youth) little recognition. Executive-level talents and gifts squandered on small tribes in Ecuador. By their energy and through inspiring others, they set up two schools, two hospitals, and many spin-off clinics and organizations.

Who will continue the tasks they began? Who will take the good news, God's love, to the world? We lack the stamina and muscles they had. Can we develop it? How?

At Grandma Kay's funeral there was one elderly friend of note. Around him, you feel like there is a fragrant cloud: the love of God. When I told "Uncle" Stu that I felt frightened and weak without his generation here to pray for us, to buffer us, he responded, "Only Jesus can supply the grace." He wrote me a letter after Will's death; I keep it in my Bible.

People like that, Grandma Kay and Uncle Stu, give courage

by their dignity and sweet example. Gentle. Tried by fire. Strong, God-fearing survivors.

To my friends, as ill prepared as I to relate to bereavement, what can I say? Now, months after Will's death, yes, it is different. The pain has lost some sharpness, but it has gone into a deeper form, a profound inner grief.

For the first three months, it was like I was on a raft in white-water rapids. Gargantuan river of pain—torrential, flooded, rocky, dangerous. But now I am in an ocean—I no longer have that moment-by-moment struggle to keep my head above water. It's calmer now. But the vastness is fearful. The sheer size of life is crushing. There is no end to all this. There seems to be no way to cross over. ("The water is wide, I can't cross over, and neither have I wings to fly/Give me a boat that can carry . . ."—a favorite ballad of Bob's.)

In the beginning you focus on minute details; you cannot see or absorb large things. Keep your hands and feet going. Eat this stuff put in front of you. Try to speak cogently. Try to rise above the gray fog swirling in your brain. Later the grayness fades, the full pain descends, and the people are gone—you are alone. But even if they were there, they cannot comprehend this. You rise; you fall. You scream (who is listening?); you cry out. The sheer loneliness of grief overwhelms you—no one is there. You are alone, drowning.

Ah, yes, Someone is there.

Someone *is* there.

That's the physical sensation: from a raging river to an endless ocean.

The spiritual sensation is of dry, Arctic cold. My life stretches ahead of me like a snow plain. Icy, empty, bleak, white, flat. I have no equipment to help me across. I can't imagine a whole lifetime of this wounded crawling. I am so angry and grumpy with the children—with Bob. Tired and sad and dry.

How do you get through? Each one's path is their own.

Just knowing that other people have made it helps, though. Others have survived this and remained sane. Do they have an inner life, or are they covering over deep wounds, repressing chaotic emotions? In defense, building a surface, shallow life? Many seem to; I cannot choose that. I will not turn away. I must find a way to grow deeper into things, not give up. I must find newness, extend old verities, grow *new* roots where needed.

After some time, you are stronger, but sorrow is still ever present.

I need Your help, Jesus, to look up to the joy and hope of *real life*. Heaven. Eternity. What is unseen. I remember our dear friend Rosa's words, "*Tenga paciencia*"—have patience. I cling to Uncle Stu's words: *Only Jesus can supply the grace.*

His earnest love, His infinite desires,
His living, endless, and devouring fires,
Do rage in thirst, and fervently require
A love 'tis strange it should desire.

We cold and careless are, and scarcely think
Upon the glorious spring whereat we drink,
Did He not love us we could be content:
We wretches are indifferent.

'Tis death, my soul, to be indifferent;
Set forth thyself unto thy whole extent,
And all the glory of His passion prize,
Who for thee lives, Who for thee dies.

THOMAS TRAHERNE

DAY One Hundred Fifty-Four

NOVEMBER 2

God, You want to re-create who I am, don't You? Grow me,
heal me from the inside out. One aspect of me You want to
address is my outlook on life, my "life view."

What is the foundational philosophy that shapes all my days?
During my twenties and early thirties I allowed myself to become
a life hater. My face looked cheerful, but in the secret place of my
heart, deep inside, I felt life was not worth the struggle. The cost is
too high, I'd murmur. At times of deepest heartache, in my
student days and as a young professional, I considered suicide (seriously enough to figure out methods). But I felt God would not
be happy to welcome me as a quitter. (Much of this is normal
artistic melancholia—I have a personality subject to extreme
highs and lows.) Some days I wanted to give up . . . give in. My
life view was very unhealthy and has been very inconsistent.

Bob's outlook on life was a major thing that attracted me to
him. On the surface, he is a pessimist—but deep inside he is
healthy! A fighter! He revels in the battle; he likes a fierce struggle. I knew we would balance each other.

Year after year, as I have gone to church, attended Bible studies, and read the Scriptures, I have never acknowledged the sin of my heart's outlook, my inner voice saying, *This life is too hard! God, You are wrong to make life so difficult and sour for us!* I seldom admitted my betrayal and was ashamed of this well-entrenched, ugly voice. I knew it wasn't good. Wasn't right. Being a life hater is completely inappropriate for someone who says she believes in God.

I have to face this now. I cannot go on saying such evil things in my spirit.

The ultimate argument against my "life is bad" view is this: Jesus gave Himself the title of *Life*. He said, "I am the . . . Life." [8] How can I continue repeating, privately, "I hate life!"?

The strange thing, the paradox, is that God has answered my crying questions. He has shown me that this world, this life, is not as He intended it to be. This is not the *Real thing*. This is the broken thing. There is a Real thing coming. This world is crying out, groaning, waiting for the revelation. [9] This is a bitter shadow of what He intended. Shadowlands.

The best and brightest things are ahead. My loved ones are there: Momcita Carlson, Dad Dick, Grandma Kay. And now Baby Will. We are on a continuum—a journey. The farther part of it—the longest part—hasn't even begun. It's ahead! *Life* as God created it, unblemished, without tarnish!! It exists, and we *will* be born into it.

It's planned for . . . hoped for . . . expected . . . *promised*.

I take that promise, Lord, for my own.

DAY One Hundred Sixty

NOVEMBER 8

When the ache of my heart overwhelms me, two things from the Bible continue to comfort me and settle me. When all else fails. In that section of the Gospels where Jesus is teaching His disciples *what* God is like and *what* the perfect Kingdom will be like, He says that God knows when those birds (for sale in the temple, priced at less than a penny apiece) fall to the ground. They were destined to die. He knows when they finally do. He pays attention.[10] He sees their death, small as they are.

He cares about the details of my life—everyone's life. Little things, big things. He knows. He's involved. He's a bird-watcher. Again and again I remember the song, "His eye is on the sparrow, and I know He watches me." This brings calmness to my heart, when the pain is a tumult.

The second thing is a fact we teach preschoolers: God gave His own Son. God's love was expressed in Jesus' dying on that "Good" Friday. Amazing. Beyond my ken. I could never have done it, but He loves *me* that much. He loves *humankind* that much. He knows all—He loves all.

Not even a sparrow,
worth only half a penny,
can fall to the ground
without your Father
knowing it. And the very
hairs on your head are all
numbered. So don't be
afraid, you are more
valuable to him than a
whole flock of sparrows.

MATTHEW 10:29-31

Simple truths help the most. Basic, "small" truths. Things we teach children. Not the complex, paradoxical topics I learned in college days. Not theology, or deep, tangled philosophy. Just simple truths for times of crisis.

Linda, dear sister-in-law, taught my kids to do something I really appreciate. When Catherine sees me crying, she is to come and give me a hug. Snuggle in my lap. Small thing, seemingly. But Catherine nurtured Will—she was his caretaker. Now, when I grieve over him, she comforts me. Little arms around my neck. Warm, wiggly body in my lap, offering love. Thank You, Lord.

Out of the heat and out of the rain,
Never to know or sin or pain,
Never to fall and never to fear,
Could we wish better for one so dear?

What has he seen and what has he heard,
He who has flown away like a bird?
Eye has not seen, nor dream can show,
All he has seen, all he may know.

For the pure powers of Calvary
Bathe little souls in innocency;
Tender, tender Thy love-words be,
Dear little child, come home to Me.

AMY CARMICHAEL

DAY One Hundred Seventy-Five

NOVEMBER 23

It's nearly six months, I guess. Catherine says Will's name daily. When I bicycled to get her at preschool, she announced to her friends, "This bike seat belonged to my William. He died. Now I sit in the bike seat." All the questions and piercing accusations Bobby skimmed through in a month or six weeks are now being rehashed in little-girl form. I feel like I'm being dragged through it all again, agonizingly slowly, over six months.

"Why weren't you watching Will, Mom? What were you doing?"

"I was working in the house, Catherine. Your dad was there outside, beside Will. Bobby was there. And our friend Amanda was there, too. He wasn't alone. I went in to answer the telephone, and then the doorbell rang, all at the same time."

It hurts, it slices my heart, hearing these questions.

I tell her what God gave me early on. It carries the ring of ultimate truth. Once during the first three months I was crying and crying in the shower, nearly hysterical, saying William's name over and over. "Oh, God, William! Oh, Will, Baby Will, William. Oh—Father God. Why didn't I put him in the high chair? Why was I so busy? Why did I take him out there, to the pool, to Bob? How could Bob watch him properly, busy cleaning the pool? I should have put him in his chair, given him something. Oh, God, *why?* Why was I so stupid? Oh, God, I took my eyes off him. *I took my eyes off him.* I took my eyes off him. How could I? How? Oh, please, please, my baby, Baby Will."

I was crazed with grief. So full of anguish. Yet there, right in that little space, I felt God speak. *You took your eyes off him. But I never did. I never lost sight of him.*

Sparrow-watcher. Son who died. Father who had the choice to give a Son, and the *power* not to give. You chose to become a bereaved Parent for me, for us, for the world. I had no choice. (If I had, I would *not* have chosen this.) You did have a choice. Life and death are in Your hands. You kept Your eye even on my littlest one. A blade of grass, a speck of sand, yet You care for him.

So that is what I tell my little girl, my middle child: "Catherine, Mommy took her eyes off of William. But Jesus never did. He never stopped looking at Baby Will." It makes me cry to tell her this. But I wipe away my tears and focus on her.

Death games are now part of my kids' lives. Death is a protagonist in the scenarios they set up. Playing with Legos, Bobby says, "This one crashes in an accident and dies." Barbie dolls, Matchbox cars, creating dinosaur land, pretend world mingling with this one. I hear Catherine say, "My grandma died. I don't have one anymore." Or Bobby: "I'm the brother in this one. I'll die." Worst of all: "She drowned."

It seems so macabre to me—ugly broken bones showing

through flesh torn and mangled. I want to rush in and say, "Stop!" Instead I listen, or I ask what is happening. I let them say what they need to say, talk as they must.

But I hate the new play.

I vow to thee, my country, all earthly things above,
Entire and whole and perfect, the service of my love:
The love that asks no question, the love that stands the
    test,
That lays upon the altar the dearest and the best;
The love that never falters, the love that pays the price,
The love that makes undaunted the final sacrifice.

And there's another country I've heard of long ago,
Most dear to them that love her, most great to them
    that know;
We may not count her armies, we may not see her
    King;
Her fortress is a faithful heart, her pride is suffering;
And soul by soul, and silently, her shining bounds
    increase,
And her ways are ways of gentleness and all her paths
    are peace.

CECIL SPRING-RICE

DAY Two Hundred Three

DECEMBER 21

William's birthday was in November. He would have been two. We went away to a cabin, offered by friends. Sally, my singer of songs, came—what a comfort. It is as if God gave her words and music to express my heart's cries. How I hate it that he's not here. Two years old. How I miss him.

We went to church in a charming white chapel in the woods. The choir was fervent but unmusical—hurt my ears, to be honest. I felt almost insulted that on William's day they could not sing better. Really, God, did they have to be bad today?

The service was difficult: I was so unhappy, sitting there. Felt exposed, vulnerable, uncovered. Jesus, are You here? Jesus, come and let us feel Your presence, please? We are in deep times: Lord, we need You!

Full of tears, full of pain.

Then as I looked at the blurry page of my Bible, I felt the Lord quietly say, *Look, Becky. See the words on this page? How many words? See all the pages in this book? How many are there?*

Now, at the far top left corner: See that single word? That's your life. A snap of the fingers. A blink of the eyes. One little word. Then it's over.

And every other word, ever after that, is glory. All GLORY.

I felt a calming peace seep through me, like warm, healing oil. Pouring truth, reality, peace. The cleanness of God's presence. Quiet, still.

It makes you want to stop complaining. Eternity is a very long time. Life is brief. If I only live a short time, even if it does have some hard days, I can be tough. Patient. A strong soldier. Not such a wimp. God, help me to have a better perspective. A longer view.

Thank You, Holy One, for hearing my cry. Thank You for touching my hurting places.

DAY Three Hundred Sixty-Six

JUNE 2

Months have passed since I've sat here and typed. Lots has happened. But internally we move slowly, still.

Bob took the day off work yesterday—the anniversary of Will's death. He hardly did that when the babies were *born!* His challenge, like that of many hardworking men, is to juggle huge demands of work and yet keep his family happy. Get the most done, in the least time. Poor man! It's tough to please your boss and still keep your wife content!

But he is managing it. Finally, we have regained joy in each other. September was the pit (at the three-month point): I was ready to divorce—if I believed in it! November? Only slightly better. Now we are happy with each other. Accepting the fact that we grieve in completely different ways. (How can he be so silent? How can he cry so little?) We respect the other person's way with pain. Give space, when one of us is lousy with anger or exhaustion. I need lots of space.

Our marriage is stronger now than it has ever been—after nine years together. We have recognized who the other person really is, no masks, no pretense. We love. We forgive. We accept one another.

Preparing for yesterday was worse than yesterday. Will May always be awful? Forever? Three weeks ago, I was in agony: bleak, black times, crying in public places for no apparent reason. Wishing someone—anyone—cared about William's death.

When the event occurs, no one can do enough—everyone expends their energy in a huge burst. All your friends and family appear, or write, or call. Then as the weeks and months drag on, and your pain only slightly lessens, most of the people disappear. You have increased your pain tolerance and are now capable of coherent thought. So things look normal, and the notes and calls from friends and family taper off. Have they forgotten? Do they not care?

Life for them has resumed its former, normal channels. For you, it will never be quite the same.

I wish people would pace themselves—spread out the attention. We received some flowers this month—some people did remember the anniversary of his death. A sprinkling of cards. Our closest friends let us know they remembered and were praying.

Deep calls to deep. Grief recognizes milestones for another's grief. Clearly, those who have suffered some sort of loss are more sensitized, and are able to reach out, even now, a year later.

My spiritual life—my relating to God—ebbs and flows. A bit weak at this point: needs attention. Every friendship has demands. On my part, I need those quiet mornings reading the wise words of poets and prophets: The Bible brings me such comfort. Study hours, listening to His loving voice. Remembering all He has given me. Singing praises to Him, in good times *and* when I'm in a bad mood. Affirming who He is, who I am. He is the Center of all, Creator; without Him there is no sense to life.

During our upcoming yearly summer trip, I need also to mend my relationship with the children. I have run here and there, neglecting them, busy and too active. Overextended.

Holy Spirit, please don't give up on me. Please show me all You want me to learn. Help me obey. Help me love the children better. They, more than anyone else, need my tenderness.

What can I say, after a year? How can I close this period of time? Perhaps all I can say is that it will never be closed. Whenever I see a white-blond-haired child of his height, whenever I kneel to offer his toys to another child, whenever his birthday comes, in some measure I will relive the loss of this most precious boy.

There will always be bruises. Arrows of joy, shafts of pain. I will always have the deepest tenderness for eighteen-month-olds. They will bring me a piercing delight, bittersweet. More pain than joy? For now, yes. As time passes, more gratitude, less grief, I imagine.

How could my love for and joy in William end? C. S. Lewis said that to love something is to be vulnerable to the greatest joy with potential for the greatest sorrow. It all hangs together.

It will not end.

My love will not end.

He said, I will forget the dying faces;
The empty places,
They shall be filled again.
O voices moaning deep within me, cease.
But vain the word; vain, vain:
Not in forgetting lieth peace.

He said, I will crowd action upon action,
The strife of faction
Shall stir me and sustain;
O tears that drown the fire of manhood cease.
But vain the word; vain, vain:
Not in endeavour lieth peace.

He said, I will withdraw me and be quiet,
Why meddle in life's riot?
Shut be my door to pain.
Desire, thou dost befool me, thou shalt cease.
But vain the word; vain, vain:
Not in aloofness lieth peace.

He said, I will submit; I am defeated.
God hath depleted
My life of its rich gain.
O futile murmurings, why will ye not cease?
But vain the word; vain, vain:
Not in submission lieth peace.

He said, I will accept the breaking sorrow
Which God to-morrow
Will to His son explain.
Then did the turmoil deep within him cease.
Not vain the word, not vain;
For in Acceptance lieth peace.

                    AMY CARMICHAEL

Where then is my hope?
Can anyone find it?
As water wears away the stones
and floods wash away the soil,
so you destroy people's hope.
If a tree is cut down,
there is hope that it will
sprout again
and grow new branches.
But when people die, they
lose all strength.
They breathe their last, and then
where are they?
My days are swifter than a
weaver's shuttle flying
back and forth.
They end without hope.

JOB 17:15; 14:19; 14:7, 10; 7:6

EPILOGUE

I am haunted by my brother's question, asked just a couple of weeks after William's death: *What brings comfort?* "I really want to know," he said. "I've asked many questions myself. What is it that helps a person weather fierce storms, and come up surviving? How can a person heal, and become productive again—not bitter, not sour?"

I have no answers. Not yet. I only know my own journey, the private lessons I've learned. I have only begun to understand William's life; his death will always hold mysteries. Until I'm there. Until I'm in the place beyond.

While grief is universal, because loss is universal, grief is also the most unique and private emotion you can experience. Pain is so personal, tied tightly to your spirit. No one else can grasp how you feel (not even your spouse) because they do not have your dreams, your background, your family set, your beliefs, your soul—whatever it is, that conglomerate of stuff that makes you *you*. Pain is solitary. So the specific things that comfort pain are particular to the individual. But I will try to set down here some of the things that have brought comfort to me.

THE REALITY OF HEAVEN
One of Bobby's books—a book for six-year-olds—comforts me; it was written by Christine Tangvald. She wanted to help

It is better to spend your
time at funerals than at
festivals. For you are
going to die, and you
should think about it
while there is still time.

Sorrow is better than
laughter, for sadness has
a refining influence on us.

A wise person thinks
much about death, while
the fool thinks only
about having a good
time now.

ECCLESIASTES 7:2-4

children who've been bereaved. The dedication is piercing and gives me bittersweet joy:

> . . . *to my wonderful parents,*
> *Harry and Frankie Harder,*
> *and to my beloved son,*
> *Thor Roald Tangvald.*
> *They have already crossed the chasm and are experiencing the*
> *reality of eternal life.*
> *Wait for me.*
> *Wait for me.*[11]

"Crossed the chasm . . . experiencing the *reality* of eternal life." Words *burned* into my heart. I see that and I cry: tears, but not acidic, tight, hurting ones. The hope implicit in that dedication opens up my spirit, claiming the reality of the other side, the place beyond. A place called heaven? Believe I will see William again? Oh, my little son, will you know me? Will you wait for me?

In my neighborhood live two lovely Muslim women who seem only nominally religious. Grieved by what religion has done to their country, they classify spiritual commitment with the uneducated, trampled lower classes. Consequently they were surprised to find me devout.

When they came to the house after William's death, their apparent lack of trust in God and their cynicism about heaven shocked me. "Be strong," they said in hushed, intense tones. "Be *strong!*"

I replied, brokenly, "I will see him again, in heaven."

They said nothing, but patted my arm in a tut-tut, old-lady

We are God's
masterpiece. He has
created us anew in Christ
Jesus, so that we can do
the good things he
planned for us long ago.

EPHESIANS 2:10

fashion. Clearly they were thinking, *Let her believe whatever will bring comfort.* Condescending, faithless.

They do not understand that a false idea cannot comfort. A bird with broken wings cannot fly. Hope can only be found in something real. Not a sugarcoated fantasy.

Solomon, who is universally considered wise, said that it is better to go to a house of mourning than to a house in festival.[12] Why? Perhaps because it makes us consider our mutability, ponder our limitations. I know that mourning has helped me to recognize heaven: to look for it and learn about it. I've been reading books, studying what people say and what Scripture teaches.

There are perhaps easier ways to find comfort, at least for the short term. Drugs and drinking are potent and effective, common avenues for escape. They dull people's pain; but they do it by dulling people's ability to feel. I've seen people become sense-*less,* in escape. Is it comforting? Must be. Does it last? Not even to the next morning.

Substances: real and tangible. Easier to grasp, for many people, than the unseen, intangible Reality of heaven. But they make one lose touch with the here and the now. You don't hurt as much, because you don't feel as much.

Heaven is not easy: It's a fierce and somewhat uncomfortable Reality. I remember the quote "The undiscovered country from whose bourne no traveller returns . . ." from Hamlet's famous soliloquy, "To be or not to be."

The unanswered Question. But it has the characteristic of truth, in that *by the light of it,* everything else becomes more clear—not less. Heaven helps us see earth more clearly.

C. S. Lewis said, "I believe in Christianity as I believe that the Sun has risen, not only because I see it, but because by it I

O Lord, by all Thy dealings with us, whether of joy or pain, of light or darkness, let us be brought to Thee. Let us value no treatment of Thy grace simply because it makes us happy or because it makes us sad, because it gives us or denies us what we want; but may all that Thou sendest us bring us to Thee, that knowing Thy perfectness, we may be sure in every disappointment that Thou art still loving us, and in every darkness that Thou art still enlightening us, and in every enforced idleness that Thou art still using us; yea, in every death that Thou art giving us life, as in His death Thou didst give life to Thy Son, our Saviour Jesus Christ. Amen.

PHILLIPS BROOKS

see everything else."[13] A favorite quote of my dad. That's sight. That's a vision of faith.

Heaven, for me, is like when the sun shines too hot and close—almost directly into your eyes, waking you. All the world is lit with light: you seem to see *inside* things.

Heaven is no myth. That is comfort.

THE TRUTH OF THE BIBLE

Another thing that brings comfort is truth: words from God. It's very fashionable among the nonreligious to mock the Bible and make fun of anyone who reads it. A lot of people are Pilate types, sarcastic and sad, who can only say, "What is truth?" But I've found that Scripture can be absolutely trusted. I love the Bible as I never did before. It's come alive for me in an enriching way.

I found that the simplest truths helped me the most. Short sentences we teach children to repeat. *God is love. God knows your name. God is good. God has all power. God has a plan for your life. God loves [insert your name]!*

Even to this day I love the babyish, most fundamental pictures. I've mentioned Luke 12 several times: the image of birds—of little value to men, of great value to God. Sold cheaply, die quickly. They are under His care. God sees little ones, nameless creatures.

Psalm 139: He knows our innermost being. Before I was born—before William was born—we were cared for. The God who is completely *other* is also the God who is completely *immanent.* Touchable. God loves *me.*

And John 3: God who created this vast universe (the intricate web of loveliness, nature unspoiled), all things under His sway, could not bear life without man. He loved *us* so much.

He allowed His Son to die. Obscene, the death of God's Child, required for the emergency reweaving of His intended union with us. He even *planned* for His Son to die (the situation was so dire—our need was so crucial). Although He wept as Jesus was killed, and the earth groaned and shook in disbelief, God held back His limitless power. He refused to intervene. He let Jesus die. He saved man.

Thus, God personally is a bereaved Parent. The unbelievable tragedy of men separated forever from God was the darkest moment in His Creation: blacker than black. The obscene spectacle of Jesus thrust up on a cross was blood-red thread woven into universal suffering—saving. God *loves* me. God suffers as I do.

Two different friends sent me quotations that mention this idea of our lives being a tapestry God is designing. "For we are His workmanship, created in Christ Jesus."[14] The threads of colors we would never choose—the colors of pain and suffering—are the very colors necessary for the particular design, our design. Our name and our identity are banded into those colors. Judy sent this:

> *My life is but a weaving*
> *Between my God and me*
> *I may not choose the colors*
> *He knows what they should be*
> *For He can view the pattern*
> *Upon the upper side*
> *While I can see it only*
> *On this the underside.*
>
> *Sometimes He weaveth sorrow*
> *Which seemeth strange to me*

But I will trust His judgment
And work on faithfully
'Tis He who fills the shuttle
He knows just what is best
So I shall weave in earnest
And leave with Him the rest.

At last when life is ended
With Him I shall abide
Then I may view the pattern
Upon the upper side
Then I shall know the reason
Why pain with joy entwined
Was woven in the fabric
Of life that God designed.
                    —Author Unknown

And our dear friend Jerry Root wrote:

> I assure you that God does not make mistakes. He doesn't
> have to back up, say "what went wrong?" and try
> again. . . . He has no new thoughts. He does not engage
> in thinking as if it were a process with a beginning,
> middle and end. He may reveal Himself logically and
> sequentially in order to funnel the glory of His eternal
> and infinite character into time and space. But God does
> not improvise. He does not have to go through either log-
> ical or sequential processes in order to come to conclu-
> sions. He has what the ancients call vision. Everything is
> always before Him; He always sees and always knows; He
> never has to acquire. Your present circumstances and the

From prayer that asks that I may be
Sheltered from winds that beat on Thee,
From fearing when I should aspire,
From faltering when I should climb higher,
From silken self, O Captain, free
Thy soldier who would follow Thee.

From subtle love of softening things,
From easy choices, weakenings,
Not thus are spirits fortified,
Not this way went the Crucified,
From all that dims Thy Calvary,
O Lamb of God, deliver me.

Give me the love that leads the way,
The faith that nothing can dismay,
The hope no disappointments tire,
The passion that will burn like fire,
Let me not sink to be a clod:
Make me Thy fuel, Flame of God.

AMY CARMICHAEL

choices before you are not the result of something catching God by surprise. They are dissident threads whose color can only be understood when seen in the context of the complete tapestry. A Master Craftsman is at work.

White and golden threads exist in our life today, mingling with the dark red-brown and black.

THE LOVE OF FRIENDS

Here again, it was the simplest, shortest messages that helped the most. Just as a mother in labor is only given basic techniques to get her through to the birth of her child (what could be more fundamental than breathing and counting, "One . . . two . . . three . . ."?), so also people in crisis need things to be *kept simple*. Almost trite—but with genuine emotion girding the sentences. Poems and verses that were sent humbly, with tears studding the pages, brought such comfort. Friends mailed short prayers or wrote gentle verses for us. A psalm, an article cut from a magazine they'd read. They did not attempt to explain deep facts about the universe—they were not smug nor did they offer know-it-all flavored words to summarize and categorize our situation.

These people were thinking of us and showed it. They tried to put themselves in our shoes. These people met a need I had: the need to know I was not cut off. Someone cared, some human hand touched mine. They reached out, sometimes clumsy, sometimes unintentionally cruel. Yet I was grateful for their attempts and tried to humbly receive what people offered. Death is a huge social taboo, and people avoid talking about it, usually. So I was comforted by their effort to bridge the gap created by my tragic situation. I was grateful

Affliction is a treasure, and scarce any man hath enough of it. No man hath affliction enough that is not matured, and ripened by it, and made fit for God by that affliction. . . . God, who is our only security.

JOHN DONNE, *Meditations, #17*

not to be *avoided*. I wanted to know I was part of the whole fabric of mankind, one thread from the entire tapestry. I belonged somewhere. Connected in the warp and weave of life.

Some good questions people asked us:

> What are you remembering today?
> What emotions are you feeling? (suggest some possibilities)
> Is there a way that I can help you?
> Do you want more meals, more baby-sitting, more silence?
> Can I get you a library book or something?

It helped when people were specific, giving a suggestion, offering a task they were willing to perform.

GREATER UNDERSTANDING OF MYSELF AND OTHERS

What other good has come from this tough year? My marriage has survived—and now thrives. (According to many books I read, this is a miracle.) I learned to forgive Bob for grieving differently. I learned to give him more space.

Bob is a wonderful person: my friend and father to my kids. He treasured William, had dreams for his life, anticipated special together-hobbies (stamp collecting for Will, coins for Catherine, rocks for Bobby). Bob suffered William's death deeply.

Although we were not companions (many books say you cannot be—that your very male/female differences separate you) we did stay parallel. We did not unplug. But unfortunately, we were not able to help each other much. The loneliest time of all.

Still, we could lie there, side by side, and know there was

someone who *nearly* felt the same as we did. Someone else grieved in the same *direction,* towards the same loss, about the same little person. We were alone, but we were not alone. The marriage survived.

Personally, I learned, perhaps too well, to set aside my tears for a more "convenient" time. I did not lay my sorrow on every passing stranger and fall apart. For an extrovert like me, who tells fellow dinner guests her life story, that's a new thing. (Self-control is not my strong point, so it's good that I learned to repress myself in something, but perhaps not good that it was with grief.)

Why is William so private and so important? I'm afraid of people's response. If I tell someone who has never lost a child, will they understand? Can they translate their area of secret pain into mine? It seems that loss is universal, but pain is individual.

The entire experience is scrambled up emotions—love mixed with pain, anger blended with fear, sorrow tinged with confusion, like a basket of colored threads tangled by a kitten's wandering paw.

You must take each color, stretch it out clearly, wind it back up, fasten it with forgiveness, and let it sit quietly, back in the basket. From time to time, you find there's another bobbin, which you didn't see, underneath the ones you've already straightened out. It's knotted and bunched up. Carefully, you work again, dividing the threads, acknowledging the source, accepting. Letting go.

It's possible to be obsessed with your own emotions, always, at all times, forever. Grief can consume every area of your life: mental, physical, spiritual, emotional. That's not healthy. Going on is a choice we make, as time passes. Neither is it correct to cover over deep wounds, saying, "I'll let time take care of it. I'll leave it to God." That denies the reality of your agony. That inhibits your growth through the pain. Grief remains a festering sore, deep underneath the surface.

Grief is self-centered, and justifiably so. But we can set grief aside, and return to it later. Both are essential, the setting aside, and the coming back. In that, over the years, comes the healing. With God's help.

A lady told me about her sister whose child died. The sister has never been the same, and is bitter and cold to many people. My friend said, "Why can't she put it behind her?"

After thinking, I responded. "She has, and that is the problem. If she remembers the child, she can love him and rejoice, after a time. It's when you, or others, never acknowledge the importance of his life and loss, that's when a person gets bitter." The flavor of pain sinks deeply into you and becomes a strong concentration over time. For good or for bad, it is distilled in you, into a life-wine, or vinegar. Others can clearly smell the fragrance, good—or not so good.

I've had times when I could see a twistedness or a tired kind of cynicism creeping into my heart. I realized I had not allowed enough space to remember. I realized I was forgetting to love William, and be thankful.

Both Pastor Jerry and many books repeat this truth: *The work of grief, good grief, is to remember.*

Remember but say nothing? Just feel everything? Don't tell the secret pain of our hearts? (And yet at other times I thrust William into a conversation. I cannot stand to have him belittled by ignoring the fact of him, dead or alive. "I have *three* children; one is dead." It makes people very uncomfortable.)

Remember but write it, don't say it? Paper has no threat. I

Even though the fig trees
have no blossoms, and there
are no grapes on the vine,
even though the olive crop
fails, and the fields lie empty
and barren, even though the
flocks die in the fields, and
the cattle barns are empty, yet
I will rejoice in the Lord!
I will be joyful in the God
of my salvation. The
Sovereign Lord is my
strength! He will make me as
surefooted as a deer and bring
me safely over the mountains.

HABAKKUK 3:17-19

can pour out my heart, say whatever I want. Many psychologists recommend "journaling" when in crisis. I did not know this. I only know it relieved me to write. Emptied me. Opened the tight hardness in my throat when I could not cry. Telling secrets in a safe place is comforting. It shines a light on fears and feelings; visible, they seem bearable. Big monsters shrink into smaller monsters? Perhaps. They don't go away, but they shrink, a little. At least mine have.

What were my monsters? I didn't know if I would divorce. I didn't know if I would have a nervous breakdown. I didn't know if my kids would make it. (How would I handle their questions? Would I go berserk?) I didn't know if I would kill myself, either in spirit (by withdrawing into a self-centered abyss), or in body (by committing suicide).

I didn't know if God would be there.

GOD ALONE IS OUR COMFORT

I think this is the most important thing I've learned so far: God is my comfort, my Comforter. In my sorrow, I *must* call on Him. Only He who inflicts the wounds can heal them. I am not given easy answers in this friendship with Him, but I find I can survive without them *when I am close to Him,* relating to Him. His presence and love comfort me, giving me strength to go on, *even with questions unresolved.*

Strangely, I need help *from* God to keep recognizing my need *of* God.

Escaping Life or Seeking God. Looking back to the time before William's death, I see patterns of behavior in my life, both good and bad. I see that my search for comfort led me to seek escape and evasion, rather than choosing to face problems head-on. In times of difficulty, rather than look to God for

Pressed out of measure and pressed to all length,
Pressed so intently, it seems beyond strength,
Pressed in the body, and pressed in the soul,
Pressed in the mind till the dark surges roll,
Pressure by foes, and a pressure by friends,
Pressure on pressure till life nearly ends.

Pressed into knowing no helper but God,
Pressed into loving the staff and the rod,
Pressed into liberty where nothing clings,
Pressed into faith for impossible things,
Pressed into living a life in the Lord,
Pressed into living a Christ-life outpoured.

AUTHOR UNKNOWN

help, I would try to solve my problems alone and comfort myself. I escaped into fantasy.

People are different in personality and taste. Some escape into television; others seek "happiness" in drugs. Sometimes alcohol brings comfort and relaxation. For still others, being in good shape becomes a mania. Some men get addicted to *Monday Night Football*.

Everyone has a place to flee for escape: Everyone needs time to rest, time to get refreshed and recharged. There's nothing wrong with that. In fact when used properly, it's a modern-day application of the Old Testament Sabbath principle. When the "miniholiday" is done, a person can go back into normal life, revitalized, energized. With a good escape, this happens. Positive outcome, a stronger, happier, well-rested individual. There are many great types of comfort and healthy uses for entertainment. However, life is not meant to be one long entertainment spree. A getaway is exactly that—time to go, and time to return.

Unfortunately, many inherently harmless escapes can easily lead to excessive, destructive habits.

Seeking relaxation is not wrong in itself; it's the excess that troubled me. Personally, I spent too much time with trivial books and beauty catalogs. I was a genuine Christian, believing in God, faithful at church, but not always applying what I knew. My time was filled with too many things, other pleasures, other comforts. I was living a roller-coaster life as a result. Too busy with too much trivia, second best.

I loved to read. Reading made me forget the things I disliked in my life; when I read, I was powerful. I lived where I wanted to in a world that I liked.

I knew I was spending an obsessive amount of time reading; I knew it was wrong for me, because its outcome was bad.

I was more irritable with the children; I was less patient with Bob. I didn't have time for my tasks at home. I was discontent with myself and my house.

The downward spiral is self-perpetuating: I fill myself up, then I feel less pleasure in God. The less pleasure I feel in Him, the more hungry and empty I am—and the more I seek comfort somewhere, anywhere. And any comfort I find is incomplete and satisfies only briefly. It's a vicious cycle. Perpetual restlessness. Continual discontent.

My escape time was not a miniholiday; it was an outer-space voyage. And I was left emotionally tired and angry that my world wasn't as effortless and simple as the world of fiction.

Something was wrong. There was clearly an imbalance some-where. But I couldn't believe my reading was the problem. *Surely it's harmless,* I thought. *Look at what other people do.* I lived in a zigzag fashion, and I wondered why my Christian life was so unsteady.

When William died, however, I didn't try to deceive myself. I knew my puny escapes would not work in this crisis. The size of the tragedy peeled layers off me, and I could see, exposed underneath, my trembling heart, vulnerable, open in the hand of God. *How?* was my biggest question. *How am I going to make it through this?* I would not find solace in anything trivial. I sepa-rated myself from everything old; I wanted only the highest and best, in me and around me. I didn't even try the old ways.

But I was desperate for something new, something genuine. Something that would really help me, comfort me.

What's So Great about Faith? I knew that anything that could bring me healing would have to be related to or from God. I believed God was real and true, and so I asked Him to help me. I turned in faith to God in this, my blackest time. I called out to God. *God Himself, personal and real, was the Answer, the something new, the something genuine.*

I've heard people say that Christians are escapists and that people lean on God because they are weak. I've also heard the same people wonder where the strength comes from to survive life's biggest crises.

Listening to them, you would think faith is a commodity, to be gotten in some mystical transaction at which they have failed. With envy in their voice, they say, *"I wish I had your faith."* Juxtaposition: They seem to pity you. Your faith is too simple; they are less gullible, less easily fooled.

I have faith—belief—in a Person, and my belief is only as good as the One I trust in. I do not have a creed or a system of behavior; it's not *a faith,* meaning I subscribe to a particular religion, boxed in with the Protestants on those neat white forms. Religion is often conventional, sometimes dead and dry. Although most of my theology is along traditional Reformed lines, the accurate words to describe me are a seeker of God, someone in a relationship with God. I am not "religious"—I am *in a relationship.*

Some people are not interested in God; they see Him as an intrusion, as someone who creates hassles for them. They do not have "faith," or trust, in God. To them, God is a miser who may have created the world, but now cramps their style. They don't think much about it; but when they do, they hope (without surety) that they'll end up in heaven (if there is one), by living a decent life. God owes them that much, at least, they believe.

Other people, in the press of normal everyday life, forget their faith. It falls by the wayside. They are so busy, they find

That is why we never give up.
Though our bodies are dying,
our spirits are being renewed
every day. For our present
troubles are quite small and
won't last very long. Yet they
produce for us an immeasur-
ably great glory that will last
forever! So we don't look at
the troubles we can see right
now; rather, we look forward
to what we have not yet seen.
For the troubles we see will
soon be over, but the joys to
come will last forever.

2 CORINTHIANS 4:16-18

themselves more and more detached from God, from church and others who believe.

In a tragedy or a time of deep crisis, people look outside themselves for answers. *Why did this happen? And to me? Are You there, God? What is going on?* Some people come back to God; others lose their "faith," feeling God was unfair to them. Their grief overwhelms them.

I believe that the "megaphone of pain," as C. S. Lewis calls suffering, draws us back into our most natural, fetal position: dependence on God. We have no choice but to recognize that we need God. Psychologists say that when a small child is hurt, the child looks automatically to the primary caregiver (usually the mother) for comfort. This is called the touchstone instinct—the child turns to its mother, and man, to God. What could be more natural, more right? Turning to the Primary Caregiver, the Life-giver, the Creator.

It's natural and appropriate to seek comfort and answers from God in a time of tragedy, but why only then? Isn't it also right to call on God with everyday questions? Are we like, or unlike, Jacob: hypocritical, charming, and greasy, but wrestling with God? Persistent in chasing God, whatever our personal failures. If we press toward God only in the darkest times, will we know how to approach Him in good times? The time of tragedy only reveals what we really are; it does not create the void in us. After the crisis has passed, will God still fit in our lives? Or do we revert to the old patterns, the old way of doing things?

I was worried about that, looking at myself, looking at others. I did not want to lose the keenness, the sharp hunger for God I had found. I had evacuated old habits and wanted to

keep them out, to stay away from them. Could I remain
focused on the new? Could it stay alive?

I must have You, Jesus. I cannot make it without You. I no longer
thought Moses, on the mountain of Sinai, was arrogant, presump-
tuous—*Let me see Your face, today, show me Your glory,* I prayed.
Otherwise, it's no good. I didn't want to go back to comforting
myself, by myself, escaping. Filling up my life with "good" things,
and leaving little room for the best, the very *best* thing: time for
God. Time with God. Friendship time.

Developing and Sustaining a Taste for God. As I pondered this
fear, I studied other people. Both in myself and others, I saw
how taste can be trained. Small children are taught to like (or
dislike) certain foods, older children mimic pop-star culture,
and adults develop an appreciation for opera. Taste can be
trained early or late; it can be impressed on a child, or acquired
in old age.

My parents gave me, early, an introduction to faith, and they
are models to me of lives well lived. Their "tastes," or values,
are selfless and lovely: a focus on spiritual things, a firm belief
that the most important things occur in the unseen world.
"The things which are seen are temporal; but the things which
are not seen are eternal."[15]

When a person presses close to God, changes begin to take
place. Priorities are adjusted and our lifestyle usually undergoes
surgery. Part of a refined "taste" involves suffering. It's not easy,
not pleasant; we can decide it isn't worth it and withdraw. Or
we can stick with the regime and increase in faith.

My parents trained me up, and later I stayed with their train-
ing. They emphasized good things: loving God, studying His
Word, low concern for physical comforts, high concern for

vigorous actions of mercy and help—toward friends and ene-
mies—these were and are evident in their daily behavior.
Laughter and humor, interactive faith speckled with energetic
kindness—these characterize their twenty-seven years as missionaries in Africa.

"Practice makes perfect" we tell children, and it's true in
Christianity, also. Faith was a "normal" part of my life—perhaps
it was, and is, a very small, unimpressive faith. But a part of me
had been cultivated, labelled, and a beginning set: *Faith.*

Real faith breathes, is organic. Only Jesus' grace brings life
to a dead faith. Alive, faith is something we can practice: it can
be developed, can grow bigger . . . just as a living muscle
grows stronger with movement. I saw active faith in my parents, and as I grew older, I tried to exercise—develop—an
active faith myself.

Not by my own insight or cleverness. I was prone to
religion, not prone to a live faith. Like many Christians, I
wanted the label, insurance for the afterlife. But evacuating
old habits made my faith come alive. *Only the comfort God
gave me satisfied and lasted.* Watching mature Christians, like
my parents, showed me the better way. *Only a living, vibrant
friendship with Him gave succor.* Nothing else. I stumbled, but
I saw the right direction to go.

"No man is an island"—John Donne's meditations, written
several hundred years ago, were favorites in my college days.
No man stands alone: each man's death diminishes me. I was
bound to be influenced by my parents' faith: I am bound to
influence others, and be strengthened or harmed by them. We
cannot separate ourselves from each other—we are tied up, and
trapped (for good or evil) in shared lives, present and past. We
are connected, linked to each other, in the chain of life.

The story is told of a youth, who lived carelessly, beginning to seriously study biology. He worked day by day watching microscopic forms developing in his laboratory. Some of these tiny living things were dying and begetting others in a brief moment of time. He rose from the microscope. "Now I see it!" he said. "I am a link in the chain, and I will not be a weak link, anymore!"

William Barclay writes, "It is our terrible responsibility that we leave something of ourselves in the world, by leaving something of ourselves in others. Sin would be a far less terrible thing, if it affected only a man, himself. The terror of every sin is that it starts a new train of evil in the world. . . . Man cannot disentangle himself from his fellow man."[16]

Either good or evil can be our inheritance. My parents have left part of themselves in me, including a strong tendency, strong links, toward faith. How grateful I am to them!!

This inheritance endured, through the black times. My center spot? Faith in God. Pennies of disbelief mingled with dollars of belief. I had resources beyond my own, and a reservoir of faith built up over time. I say this, noting humbly that it's a gift from God, and available to anyone. All we have to do is ask, genuinely wanting faith.

If we ask, we will *always* get something. That's a promise. We may get more than we bargained for . . . God is in the process of growing humans into a larger size. He is not willing to have us immature, forever. He wants true children, true miniature Christ-ones. Part of our development includes His permission for, His allowance of, pain in our lives, darkness woven into the pattern, not only ease and light.

At times it is bleak: An amputation or severe pruning of a tree leaves gaps in the branches for a season, or even longer.

But He created us and knows us intimately: He measures every part of us, and sees our temperament and strength: He gauges every drop of pain, and says, "This far, no further!"

The miracle is that He does not leave us alone. *He does not leave me alone.* He watches each step, carefully.

May my pain in my loss of William, may my joy at the memory of William, always draw my attention to You, Lord God.

May I not pull away from Your hand, whether the task is surgery and pruning, or flowering, harvesttime.

Much time has passed. Some poems and prayers seem a vital part of my heart now. Gleaned, gathered in, from hours of good reading, the inheritance of godly and gifted authors; they inspire and uplift.

Among my favorites are C. S. Lewis, Amy Carmichael, Isobel Kuhn, Elisabeth Elliot and Betty Scott Stam—Christians whose lives I admire particularly, whose writings give substantive help. Long ago, in a talk she gave, Elisabeth Elliot referred to a prayer by Betty Scott Stam, which is especially precious and filled with passionate abandon to God.

Not merely a wonderful prayer of commitment, this is also a great barometer of spiritual health, revealing the state of my heart. If I can pray this prayer, really meaning it, all is well. If I find I choke, or hesitate at some point, or my impulse is to avoid saying it at all—then I know I need to examine myself. I check: What am I holding back? Where am I afraid? What's wrong?

Praying for help, I ask God to show me, search me, know my heart (Psalm 139). I confess my true feelings, and tell Him to take away whatever I am placing between us. I ask Him to forgive me, to help me start again. Then, freely, I pray this prayer:

> *Lord, I give up all my own purposes and plans . . .*
> *and accept Thy will for my life.*
> *I give myself, my life, my all utterly to Thee*
> *to be Thine forever. . . .*
> *Fill me and seal me with Thy Holy Spirit.*
> *Work out Thy whole will in my life,*
> *at any cost, now and forever.*
> *Amen.*[17]

APPENDIX

Forgiveness

Forgiveness is a big topic, and we primarily think of it in theological terms, how God has forgiven us. What Jesus in His perfection did for us. How does it enter into this book? What part does it have in William's death and our life afterwards?

FORGIVING EACH OTHER

I suppose the obvious answer would be between Bob and me. In basic terms, Bob was there, at the pool, when William fell in, and I was not. Until this year, probably in my deepest heart I believed Bob was more negligent than I. After all, he was there. The newspaper printed a cruel skeleton of our story in these black-and-white terms.

But it's not that simple. I was the one who took William outside; I put him in the danger zone.

Our recent talks about this book brought up memories we had never spoken about before in detail. We had never discussed *exactly* our memories of that day.

As he read the final edits of this book, Bob said, "You left some things out. It's not totally accurate."

"What do you mean?"

"You softened what happened by the pool."

"I did not. That's what I remember!"

"Becky, I did not just *ask* you not to leave William—we had a *fight*. I *pleaded* with you."

"I don't remember that."

"You don't remember me saying to you, 'He's losing his fear of water'?"

"No, I don't remember that."

A long pause in our conversation.

As the realization dawned on me, I said aloud, "You would never say something like this to me, unless it's true." I trust Bob's memory more than mine. And as I painfully re-create and try to relive those moments, some of that phrase jangles in my memory. Not clearly. Not exactly as he says. But enough. And with horror I realize he is right.

For three years I forgot exactly what he said and how he said it. I suppose that is some kind of grace or mercy of God. Dealing with it three years later is hard enough; how would I have survived if I had remembered it perfectly?

Forgiveness. Bob has had to let go and forgive me. He had asked me not to leave William, *begged* me. He knew he couldn't pay proper attention to him, but I refused to listen.

Sometimes it seems like there's a small lingering flavor of blame, still, in his fear for Bobby and Catherine and their safety.

In my opinion, Bob has had to carry the heavier load of pain. He held William's body fresh from the water—cold, dead weight. God protected me, putting Bob in a harder position. That feeling is imprinted forever, I imagine—a wet, limp body in his powerless arms.

Did William call? Did he try to reach for his dad, or his brother, as he tripped over? Those questions haunted Bob, made him weep, months later.

FORGIVING WILLIAM

An even stranger aspect of dealing with the death of a loved one is learning to forgive him. For dying. For leaving you behind.

At one point, in one of my "screaming rides" in the car, I found myself saying, "Why did you go, William? Oh, William, come back. Don't leave me, Baby Will!"

And I was afraid.

I realized there was a part of me that blamed him for dying. For going away. I had to forgive him for leaving me behind. Going ahead of me, to heaven. It's not rational, but emotions do not always make sense. But the emotions are real and need to be faced, acknowledged.

FORGIVING MYSELF

If someone had said to me before William's death, "You cannot be perfect. And your mothering will not be perfect," I would have wholeheartedly agreed and never questioned this statement. But we all hope we can protect our children, at least physically—this seems to be within our control. We spend lots of money and time "childproofing" our homes to ensure their safety.

But we failed. William fell into our own pool. I had to forgive myself for not being there when he fell in.

I struggle to forgive myself for overruling Bob's caution. To this day, I look back and wrestle.

Harriet Sarnoff Schiff's book *The Bereaved Parent* helped a great deal, in this as in other things. She said, "Try to understand and accept the concept that perfect parenting is a role beyond human capability."[18] Her chapter on guilt and bereavement set my heart free from some of the trapped feeling I had in the early months after William's death. A part of me had blamed me, still does.

Accidents happen; I have to accept that he could have died any number of ways, and that I did not have control, absolute control, over the safety of my child. Over any of my family. This is excruciating—and frightening—to accept. Sometimes the world looks like an evil monster, waiting to gobble up my remaining loved ones. Fear goes, and fear returns. Forgiveness, guilt, fear, and grief are in flux; they ebb and flow.

If one could perfectly re-create a scene of death, there could be clarity on blame. Especially this kind of death. In the final analysis, three years later, I have to say that I am more to blame than Bob. But this is not something that can be faced calmly, easily. You could go insane if you dwell on it. I cannot let myself linger here or the pain surfaces, unbearable. This will take time to process—much time.

FORGIVING GOD

The strangest, most peculiar thing is having to forgive God.

Please don't misunderstand. I am not saying God sins, and we grandly offer Him mercy. I am saying that because there is an emotional cutting and hurting, which God could have prevented, you must forgive. He had the power to forbid the pain, the death. He did not.

So there is a feeling similar to forgiveness that you must offer up to Him. It's really not forgiveness at all; it's acceptance. But the flavor and taste and action of it in your heart are exactly the same as when you forgive a fellow man.

That's an extremely important step.

Ultimately we must say to God, "You have permission to do as You see best." God has already done so. He has already killed (by absence of intervention), or allowed the death of, the one you love. You offer your hand of friendship, in spite of this. It feels like you are forgiving God.

That's an emotional "forgiveness" we offer God. There is also an intellectual struggle, in forgiving life, wrestling with the "unfairness" of things.

I appreciate Rabbi Kushner's book, *When Bad Things Happen to Good People,* and I especially admire his personal warmth and caring for bereaved readers. I found his philosophy helpful in one particular way: He tolerates ambiguity. He argues that a lack of resolution can itself be a type of resolution. Acceptance, not resignation. He advises people to go beyond the question *why.* To go on and choose to live with unanswered questions.

In my university days we studied the dilemma "How can a God of love allow suffering? Either He is not good, or else He lacks power to forbid the suffering."

According to Rabbi Kushner, God cannot shield us from suffering. God is not actually the complete master of all, but more like the kind of god ancient Greeks had in their mythology, with limits and deficits. God has perfect goodness and is loving, but He is not omnipotent, Kushner says. God cannot forbid the pain, the death, because He is trapped in the laws of the world He created. He is not able.

Looking back at William's death, I believe this view of God is too small. I remember learning about a third option, one that leaves God all of His might and power and still claims He is good and just. Explanation number 3 says that God allows the evil circumstances of a broken world to touch even His beloved ones, even "good people." It is permitted.

God does not intervene to change all natural consequences.

He does not suspend the law of gravity for me. He allows evil to come, even to a much-loved child.

However, He will walk through the evil beside us. He will not abandon us, but will draw us into His presence. He drew me. At times I felt so alone, cut off from other human beings, isolated and almost cursed. At those times I turned to God, crying out for help.

At times even God seemed distant—I can't pretend there was always an instant warmth and magical response. Was I too numb to feel His presence? All my emotions were wrapped up in grieving over William. Was my grief building a chasm between God and me? I believe God watched me, measuring my strength, tending me as a gardener watches a beloved tree after severe pruning. He cannot be less faithful than a loving mother over the crib of a fevered child. The child, fighting pain and fear, is not always aware, but the parent *never leaves* the child's side.

God had power to intervene, but He used His power to carefully tailor each circumstance surrounding William's death rather than to forbid them altogether. He allows me pain, sometimes great pain, for a short time, this brief time of my short life. It is permitted.

Resignation is passive and without hope. *Acceptance* is active and filled with expectation. I want to be the kind of person who expects good things from life. God permitted the pain in my heart, and I must give Him permission to do whatever He wills. A paradox of peace.

Rabbi Kushner has fealty to God, and he concludes chapter 5 with clear perspective on the meaning of life, quoting a fellow believer: "We owe God our lives. . . . We have the duty to worship Him and do as He commands us. That's what we're here on earth for, to be in God's service, to do God's bidding."[19]

That kind of loyalty gives comfort and strength. Like a pilgrim on a journey, I expect some rough roads and valleys of darkness. Perhaps we should ask *why* when the way is flower-strewn, rather than taking our prosperity for granted! Plato said, "The unexamined life is not worth living." All too often, we live an easy but shallow life, unthinking.

Do easy lives cause us to forget what life is all about? It seems so. We are prone to superficiality when comfortable. Depth comes from pain.

Christianity teaches that this life span is short. My sixty or eighty years here is actually a dress rehearsal for the real performance. There is life after death. The Bible says this world is not our home; we are strangers and pilgrims trapped for a time on a battlefield of good and evil. Real Life is ahead, and real Home is beyond what we see.

When we accept pilgrim status, we see God in all things, whether we are running playfully in the sunlight or fighting in the darkness. Our steady progress forward, in both, comes from looking to God for love and strength and purity. In both, we fix our eyes outside and up, beyond our circumstances.

At a time of a personal loss and great agony, this is not a simple thing. You cannot find emotional comfort in a mantra, mumbling, "Pilgrim . . . journey . . . hard times . . ." A mantra only teaches you how to be numb, resigned.

In great sorrow, you become like a little child. The only comfort you find is in the arms of your strong Parent. The only relief you feel is tracing the tears down His face, hearing your sobs echo in His. "He who did not spare His own Son . . ."

The Cross of God's Son answered my questions. All my

What can we say about
such wonderful things as
these? If God is for us,
who can ever be against
us? Since God did not
spare even his own Son
but gave him up for us
all, won't God, who
gave us Christ, also give
us everything else?

ROMANS 8:31-32

grumbling stopped when I looked there; all my confusion was stilled. I could not doubt that God loved me, looking at what He did for me. I might not understand why and how, in my particular life, at a specific time, certain things happened. But I knew He cared. I knew He wept with me.

The Cross is my answer to the question of my suffering. It's not an easy, packaged answer; it does not add up like a simple two-plus-two equation. The Cross satisfies our questions because the suffering there is bigger than all other pain. The Cross shows me God's heart. When that's revealed, and when I'm really looking, I can wait. I can trust. I find patience for unresolved questions, looking at the size of His love.

Children and Grief

Helping my children deal with William's loss was a huge challenge. The most helpful thing I learned in the first year was how at different ages, children think and perceive differently. I needed ideas appropriate to their ages, six and three. My pastor's wife, Dottie, and a former neighbor, Leigh, also kept a lookout for articles and books on children and grieving. They were an invaluable resource, helping me to help my little ones.

GRIEF AT AGE THREE

Catherine (age three) could only think in very concrete terms. She needed to be told how permanent and final our loss was. However, at first, I could not phrase it that way. It hurt too much. And so I hindered her understanding the finality of William's death.

Speaking to Catherine, I paraphrased a book that was perfect for Bobby at age six: *Someone I Love Died* by Christine Tangvald. I said, "You and I have an inside part and an outside part, don't we, Catherine? Your outside part used to be little, and you could not walk or talk. You were just a baby. But now your outside part, your body, is big, and you can put your own clothes on, and eat your food alone, and all kinds of things.

"Well, your inside part didn't really change—the part of you that makes you Catherine. We call it a soul and spirit. It was there when you were born, it was there when you were little, and now that you are a big three-year-old girl, your soul is still there inside you. And it will be the same, when you are very, very old.

"When William died, his outside part, his body, stopped breathing. His heart didn't go *bump-bump* anymore. But William's inside part is still alive—the bit of him which never changes in size, his soul, is still alive. And that part of him loves you still, and that part of him lives in heaven now. We will see him again, someday, Catherine. We will see him again."

She understood what I had said, and so although she missed him, she did not have terror and massive grief. She didn't really express sorrow until months had passed. She believed that when I said we'll see him again I meant in a few weeks, or a month. I had to keep telling her it would not be for a very, very long time.

She'd wake up to each new day, thinking of him.

She'd wake up asking for him.

To her, the night was a long, long time. An *entire day* was a very long time indeed. So perhaps enough of that longness meant *this was the day.*

"Mommy, will we see William? Is this the day?" Day after day, she kept asking. (She voiced my heart's hunger.)

"No, not today. No, Catherine." (Saying it broke a part of me, each time.)

Finally I said, "It won't happen until you are old, even older than Mommy. Then you'll see William again." At that point, I think, her grief began in earnest. At that point her questions and issues became more intense.

I welcomed her yearning for William. I didn't want her to be hurting, but I knew how much she had loved him, and I saw it

as normal and right. I cherished those daily, weekly questions.
A part of me sorrowed as the months lessened the mention of
his name on her lips. I blessed every mention of his name.

GRIEF AT AGE SIX

Catherine's and Bobby's timing was very different, and that
helped me a lot because if they had both suffered at once,
I think it would have broken me. But it was hard to answer the
same questions over and over. It hurt.

Bobby confronted many issues early on. He was the first one
to see William dead. He screamed to Dad, reached in, and
began pulling him out of the water.

William was so heavy that Bobby could not lift him fully,
and he partially dropped him. A week later, Bobby asked me,
"Mom, did I hurt him, when he slipped from my arms as I
lifted him? He bumped the ground."

"No, Bobby. He was gone already. He could not feel anything,
anymore, in his body."

Bobby asked, "Mom, when I said good-bye to him in the
hospital, he was warm. How did the doctors know he was
dead? Are we sure?"

"Yes, Bobby, he was warm. But his heart wasn't beating. His
brain had stopped. They can see brain waves, when you are
alive, on those special machines. The reason he was warm again
was because the nurses and other medical people had been
working on his body for so long. They checked many times,
hoping his heart would beat again. They never saw anything,
no blips."

Bobby wanted to know what we did with William's body.
At first I was afraid to tell the children that we had had
William's body cremated. I generalized. I said that most of the

time when people die, they are put in a nice box, a coffin, in the ground. Then we put a large cross, or an angel-shaped stone, or a square stone over the place, with their name on it. That's what those things are that we see in the cemetery.

Bobby is too smart. He didn't miss a trick.

Later he queried me. "We didn't do that with William, did we, Mom?"

I looked around to see if Catherine was within earshot. She wasn't.

"No, Bobby. Sometimes people put the body into a very hot fire, and they turn the body into ashes. Then you have a beautiful brass box or an urn with the ashes inside. But, Bobby, their inside part, their soul, isn't there anymore. That part of William that is alive still loves you, still thinks of you. It's only his body that's turned into ashes."

LETTING THEM ACT THEIR AGE

Both kids were awful at William's memorial service. I remember feeling angry that no one was helping me "entertain" them when all I wanted was to focus on the service. Part of me was furious that they could not sit still, completely still, at this time of all times. But my rational part knew they hadn't had much practice sitting quiet and still in grown-up meetings. Our church held Sunday school for the children during morning worship, and they hardly ever went into the sanctuary. I was able to let it go.

I tried to place no prohibitions on the ways the children dealt with William's death. They were allowed to say anything, ask anything, play any games (including drowning ones), sing any songs. Emotionally, I closed no doors and locked no cupboards. Nothing was off-limits. They could search my heart and theirs freely without fear of disapproval. They were allowed to ask bizarre or painful questions.

This was very expensive for me emotionally. At times, my heart screamed out, "No, don't say that!" At times I had to maintain a calm front, a bland exterior, when inside I was boiling over with pain or rebellion—against their normal childish processes. It really, really hurt. I hated the way dying was now a part of our everyday life.

For example, they would introduce death into most days' activities, as part of their dialogue or play. Some Matchbox car would crash; some Barbie character would die. Or else, when they told stories (we always tell each other stories), one protagonist would have a funeral.

It was difficult to allow them freedom in this. Yet I knew instinctively that they must circle around this concept, wrestle with it on their own terms, and pin it down, in order to remember William, and in order to move forward to the future.

Suggested Reading

FOR CHILDREN

Christine Harder Tangvald, *Someone I Love Died* (Colorado Springs, Colo.: David C. Cook, 1988)

Carolyn Nystrom, *Emma Says Goodbye* (Elgin, Ill.: Lion Publishing, 1990)

Bryan Mellonie & Robert Ingpen, *Lifetimes: The Beautiful Way to Explain Death to Children* (New York: Bantam, 1983)

FOR ADULTS

Author's note: Books are listed in order of my preference.

Joseph Bayly, *Heaven* (Colorado Springs, Colo.: David C. Cook, 1987)

————, *The Last Thing We Talk About* (Colorado Springs, Colo.: David C. Cook, 1969)

Granger E. Westberg, *Good Grief* (Minneapolis: Augsburg Fortress, 1962)

Elisabeth Elliot, *A Path Through Suffering* (Ann Arbor, Mich.: Servant, 1990)

Harriet S. Schiff, *The Bereaved Parent* (New York: Viking Penguin, 1978)

John Bramblett, *When Good-Bye Is Forever: Learning to Live Again After the Loss of a Child* (New York: Ballantine, 1991)

Nicholas Wolterstorff, *Lament for a Son* (Grand Rapids, Mich.: Eerdmans, 1987)

Therese A. Rando, *How to Go on Living When Someone You Love Dies* (New York: Bantam, 1991)

Margaret B. Spiess, *Cries from the Heart: Prayers for Bereaved Parents* (Grand Rapids, Mich.: Baker Book House, 1991)

Luci Shaw, *God in the Dark: Through Grief and Beyond* (Grand Rapids, Mich.: Zondervan, 1993)

Catherine Marshall, *Light in My Darkest Night* (New York: Avon, 1990)

J. Oswald Sanders, *Heaven Better by Far* (Grand Rapids, Mich.: Discovery House, 1993)

Anthony Guest, *Little Book of Comfort* (San Francisco: Harper San Francisco, 1993)

Dan Schaefer & Christine Lyons, *How Do We Tell the Children: A Parents' Guide to Helping Children Understand and Cope When Someone Dies* (New York: Newmarket Press, 1988)

BOOKS I WISH I'D FOUND SOONER

Jill Worth, *When a Baby Dies* (U.K.: Hodder & Stoughton, 1995)

Joni Eareckson Tada, *Heaven* (San Francisco: Harper San Francisco, 1995)

Carla K. McClafferty, *Forgiving God* (Grand Rapids, Mich.: Discovery House, 1995)

Paula D'Arcy, *Song for Sarah* (Wheaton, Ill.: Harold Shaw, 1979)

Paul W. Nisly, *Sweeping Up the Heart: A Father's Lament for His Daughter* (Intercourse, Penn.: Good Books, 1992)

Elizabeth Kübler-Ross, *Death: The Final Stage of Growth* (New York: Simon & Schuster, 1986)

Henri J. Nouwen, *The Wounded Healer: Ministry in Contemporary Science* (New York: Doubleday, 1979)

ACKNOWLEDGMENTS

Many, many people played a part in making this book possible. Warm and heartfelt gratitude goes to:

All of our friends, and friends of friends, who showered us with kindness in the form of calls, letters, flowers, and caring acts, big and small. You helped us make it through each day.

Our church in California, Peninsula Hills Presbyterian Church. You cradled us in your arms, and we all grew up a little bit more together.

College Church in Wheaton, Illinois, and especially to Kent Hughes and Larry Fullerton. You reached out to us across the miles, and we feel your love still.

Jerry Root. You came for us. We are in your debt.

My brother Peter. Your question sparked this book.

Dan Elliott, for his encouragement and professional advice.

My editor at Tyndale House, Kathy Olson—sensitive, firm, encouraging: I could not have done it without you. Your quilting work made this a book!

My kids. I love you. Your loss was too big to process. We are not done yet.

My husband, Bob, a private man who has allowed me to shout our story to the world.

NOTES

----

1. Matthew 5:45.
2. Psalm 23:4.
3. Helmut Thielicke, *Death and Life* (Philadelphia: Fortress Press, 1970), xxv–xxvi; quoted in Joseph Bayly, *The Last Thing We Talk About* (David C. Cook, 1969), 107–108.
4. Joseph Bayly, *The Last Thing We Talk About* (David C. Cook, 1969), 20.
5. Bayly, 24.
6. Elisha A. Hoffman, "I Must Tell Jesus."
7. Bayly, 116.
8. John 14:6.
9. Romans 8:18-22.
10. Luke 12:6-7; Matthew 10:29-31.
11. Christine Harder Tangvald, *Someone I Love Died* (David C. Cook, 1988).
12. Ecclesiastes 7:2.
13. C. S. Lewis, "Is Theology Poetry?" *The Weight of Glory and Other Addresses* (New York: Macmillan, 1980), 92.
14. Ephesians 2:10.
15. 2 Corinthians 4:18.
16. Daily Study Bible: The Letter to the Romans (Louisville: Westminster/John Knox Press, 1975), 186.
17. Betty Scott Stam, *The Faith of Betty Scott Stam in Poem and Verse* (New York: Fleming H. Revell Co., 1938), 2.

18. Harriet S. Schiff, *The Bereaved Parent* (New York: Viking Penguin, 1978), 44.

19. Harold S. Kushner, *When Bad Things Happen to Good People* (New York: Avon, 1983), 93.